Effective
Presentation Skills

Enhance presentation performance by acquiring practical presentation and language skills. Deliver powerful message, win business and improve results.

CARROT HOUSE

CARROT HOUSE
P.O.Box #2924, St. Marys, Ontario, Canada

Effective Presentation Skills
© Carrot House

All rights reserved. No part of this publication may be reproduced, stored in a retrieval system, or transmitted in any form or by any means without the prior permission in writing of Carrot House.

Printed January 2020

Author: Carrot Language Lab

ISBN 978-89-6732-040-9

Printed and distributed in Korea
9th Fl., 488 Gangnam St., Gangnam-gu, Seoul, South Korea 06120

Curriculum Map

Course	Level 1	Level 2	Level 3	Level 4	Level 5	Level 6	Level 7	Text Book
General Conversation	Essential English : Begin Again / Pre Get Up to Speed 1~2	New Get Up to Speed+ 1~2	New Get Up to Speed+ 3~4	New Get Up to Speed+ 3~4	New Get Up to Speed+ 5~6	New Get Up to Speed+ 7~8		
	Daily Focused English 1	Daily Focused English 2						
Discussion				Active Discussion 1	Active Discussion 2	Dynamic Discussion	Dynamic Discussion	
			Chicken Soup Course	Chicken Soup Course	Chicken Soup Course	Chicken Soup Course		
				Dynamic Information & Digital Technology	Dynamic Information & Digital Technology	Dynamic Information & Digital Technology		
Business Conversation	Pre Business Basics 1	Pre Business Basics 2	Business Basics 1	Business Basics 2	Business Practice 1	Business Practice 2		
Global Biz Workshop				Effective Business Writing Skills (Workbook)	Effective Business Writing Skills (Workbook)			
				Effective Presentation Skills (Workbook)	Effective Presentation Skills (Workbook)			
					Effective Negotiation Skills (Workbook)	Effective Negotiation Skills (Workbook)		
					Cross-Cultural Training 1~2 (Workbook)	Cross-Cultural Training 1~2 (Workbook)		
					Leadership Training Course (Workbook)	Leadership Training Course (Workbook)		
Business Skills			Simple & Clear Technical Writing Skills	Simple & Clear Technical Writing Skills				
			Effective Business Writing Skills	Effective Business Writing Skills				
			Effective Meeting Skills	Effective Meeting Skills				
			Business Communication (Negotiation)	Business Communication (Negotiation)				
			Effective Presentation Skills	Effective Presentation Skills				
				Marketing 1	Marketing 1			
						Marketing 2		
						Management		
On the Job English				Human Resources	Human Resources	Human Resources	Human Resources	
				Accounting and Finance	Accounting and Finance	Accounting and Finance	Accounting and Finance	
				Marketing and Sales	Marketing and Sales	Marketing and Sales	Marketing and Sales	
				Production Management	Production Management	Production Management	Production Management	
				Automotive	Automotive	Automotive	Automotive	
				Banking and Commerce	Banking and Commerce	Banking and Commerce	Banking and Commerce	
				Medical and Medicine	Medical and Medicine	Medical and Medicine	Medical and Medicine	
				Information Technology	Information Technology	Information Technology	Information Technology	
				Construction	Construction	Construction	Construction	
		Construction English in Use 1 ~ 4	Construction English in Use 1 ~ 4					
		Public Service English in Use	Public Service English in Use					

※ This Curriculum Map illustrates the entire line-up of textbooks at CARROT HOUSE.

Introduction

Carrot House Methodology

Andragogical Approach & Productive English

The teaching of children (pedagogy) and adult learning (andragogy) are distinctively different. Pedagogy is akin to training and encourages convergent thinking and rote learning. It is compulsory, centered on the teacher and the imparting of information with minimal control by the learner. Andragogy, by contrast, is about education as freedom. It encourages divergent thinking and active learning. It is voluntary, learner oriented and opens up vistas for continuing learning. Adults need to feel independent and in control of their learning. Therefore, Carrot House curriculum is based on andragogy and is designed to encourage learners' participation and engagement by providing more task-based activities and opportunities to frequently interact in the classroom.

People want to achieve communicative competence when they learn other languages. English education in EFL environments has been rather focused on the receptive skills of English—listening and reading—which simply increases learners' knowledge about a language, not the competence of using it. If people are well equipped with productive skills—speaking and writing—they will be competent in English communication.

This is why Carrot House curriculum is designed to enhance learners' productive skills throughout the course. This andragogical approach of the Carrot House Curriculum, which focuses on productive English, will enable learners to achieve communication skills necessary for global competence. Carrot House's teaching philosophy and curriculum combine to provide a "Language for Success" for all learners.

Communicative Language Learning (CLL)

This communicative interaction, the essential component of language acquisition, does not occur in a typical, non-meaningful, fun-oriented conversation with native speakers. It occurs in a negotiated interaction through which a well-trained teacher provides the comprehensible input that is appropriate to the learners. The learners, at the same time, actively utilize the opportunities given to them by the teachers.

To this end, the Communicative Language Learning (CLL) method is employed in the field of Foreign Language Acquisition. The CLL method provides activities that are geared toward using language pragmatically, authentically and functionally with the intention of achieving meaningful purposes.

Lesson Composition & User's Guide

Overview

Effective Presentation Skills is intended to improve learners' business presentation skills by acquiring language and presentation skills. This book is composed of total of 5 parts

① FYI: Background Knowledge   ② Language Focus   ③ Presentation Build-up: 3 Steps   ④ Review   ⑤ Presentation On Stage

FYI: Background Knowledge provides learners with information about the essentials of presentations. The information covers a wide spectrum from ways to effectively craft presentations, present key concepts, use visuals effectively and ways to capture the audience. Language Focus helps learners to employ a variety of expressions that strengthen their presentation speaking. Presentation Build-Up:3 Steps provides learners with real-life presentation context and 2 presentation cases. Learners can use 3 steps to brainstorm, compare good/bad presentation cases and to benchmark for his or her own presentation. The review section allows learners and instructors to check if all the learning objectives of the lesson have been met. Presentation On Stage is the main activity part of the lesson and requires the learners to create a presentation and present as if in real-time. This part is designed as teacher-independent so that it can provide learners with opportunities to use the acquired knowledge and language in the lesson in a practical way.

Section 1   You Learn How To

The "You learn how to" section provides learning objectives at the beginning of each lesson. These precise learning objectives facilitate learner's ability to learn new skills. Each lesson is composed of 3 skills that the learners will be able to achieve by the end the lesson. In this regard, the instructor should check whether the objectives have been met at the completion of a lesson.

Section 2   Getting Started

This part induces creativity on the learner's part. Learners will use the image in the title page to answer questions creatively; they are also asked to present their ideas. The image does not necessarily relate to the unit's theme; therefore instructors can use this time as an ice-breaker for class.

Section 3   Warm-up Questions

Each unit begins with 3 warm-up questions. These questions help stimulate learners' thinking before getting into the unit. These open-ended questions are related to the unit's topic and can be used to initiate discussions in class. These questions should not be heavily discussed, rather only be used to introduce unit's topic and help learners to feel at ease before entering the unit.

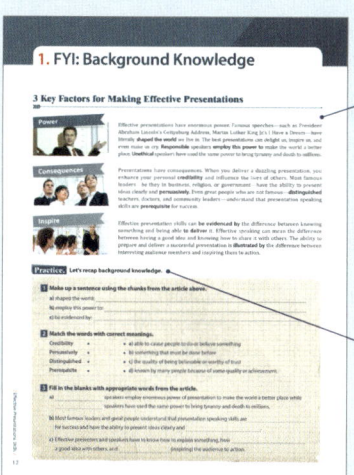

Section 4   FYI: Background Knowledge

• Background Knowledge Reading

Each unit provides different background knowledge about the essentials of giving effective presentations. Such information includes ways to effectively craft presentations, present key concepts, use visuals effectively and ways to capture the audience. Due to advanced level of reading, it is best recommended that the instructor pre-study and review this section before going into the class. It is important for the instructors to understand the key concepts of the article and be able to articulate the main ideas to the class. Instructors can decide to do a class reading or a self reading and facilitate class discussion on idea-sharing. Since the purpose of this section is to layout the ground for the unit, it should not be too heavily focused. Just making sure that the learners understand the information and the concepts in the article should be sufficient.

• Practice. Let's Recap Background Knowledge

This section is used to check learner's comprehension on knowledge background reading. Practice includes reviewing expressions/terms as well as activity for checking understanding of the article above. Instructors can decide to make this section as a class practice activity or a self practice activity. The correct answers for the practice activity are provided at the back of the book. It is recommended that the instructor check the answer together with the class.

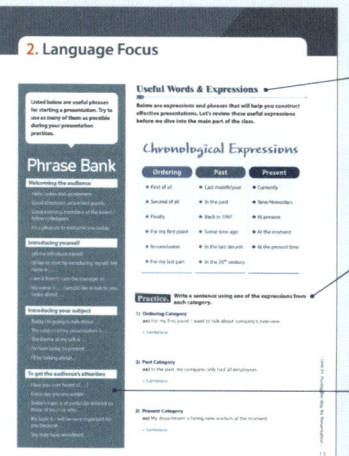

Section 5   Language Focus

• Useful Words and Expressions

This section of the book provides the learners with useful words and key expressions that can be used to make effective presentations. The theme for these words and expressions differ for all units. The instructor should read and go over all the words and expressions together with the class.

• Practice Activity

This practice section is used to review useful words and expressions learned previously. It usually is composed of 1 review activity that are either matching, choosing the right answer, or fill in the blanks questions. The instructor can decide to make this a class practice activity or a self-practice activity. The correct answers are provided at the back of the book and it is recommended that the instructor go over the answer together with the class.

Section 6   Phrase Bank

All units include phrase bank. Phrase bank provides useful expressions and patterns that can be used in presentations. The phrases are related to the unit's theme and the instructor should go over the phrases together with the class. Many times, learners are used to using same expressions and phrases, so the goal of the phrase bank is to encourage learners to use newly acquired phrases here. In particular, the phrase bank will reappear in "Presentation On Stage" part, and the learners check to see if they have utilized the phrases in their presentation or not. The instructor should read and practice the phrases together with the class.

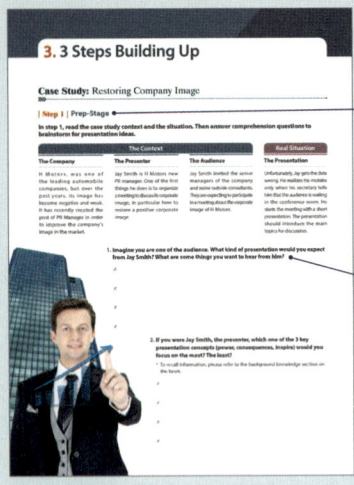

Section 7 — Building Up Presentation-3 Steps

① **Step 1: Prep-stage**   ② Step 2: The Cases   ③ Step 3: Follow-Up

• **Step 1: Prep-Stage**
Step 1 provides context and information for real-life case presentation. The context, related to the unit's theme is given from the company, the presenter and the audience's point of view. These contexts set the stage for practicing presentation in the next step (step 2). Learners are asked to brainstorm and share ideas about the given context. As the first step for making presentation, it is crucial for instructors to make sure learners understand the context.

• **Comprehension Questions**
After reading the case study context, learners are asked to answer 2 comprehension questions. These questions require learners to make connections between background knowledge section and the case study context. The purpose of these questions is to stimulate learner's thinking process and to help them relate theoretical and practical aspects of presentation. The instructor should go over questions and ask learners to share the answers with the class. For this part of the lesson, it is important for learners to listen to as many different ideas and opinions as possible.

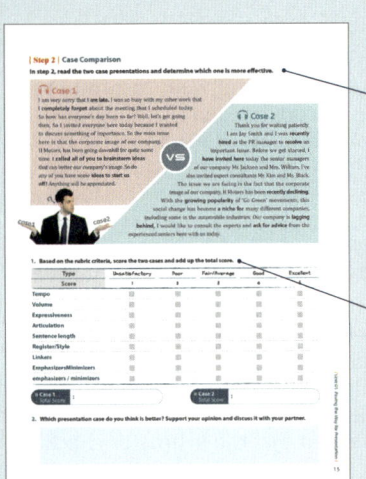

Section 8 — Building Up Presentation-3 Steps

① Step 1: Prep-stage   ② **Step 2: The Cases**   ③ Step 3: Follow-Up

• **Step 2: Case Comparison**
This section provides 2 cases 2 presentations based on the context given in step 1. Most of the time 1 case shows good example of an effective presentation and the other case shows bad example of ineffective presentation. There is a MP3 for the cases where learners can listen to a native speaker present each case. If available, the instructor can decide to play the MP3 in class or have learners read the cases on their own. The instructor should not inform the learners which case is bad or good. Let the learners discuss on their own; they will also be asked to score the cases in the next section.

• **Case Study Checklist**
This checklist helps learners to assess the cases to determine whether it is an unsatisfactory, poor, average/fair, excellent presentation. The excellent case presentation should incorporate information from background knowledge reading, words/expressions from language focus and use formal English. Essentially, the checklist will act as a guideline to writing an effective presentation. In this section have learners score the two cases and share their thoughts with a partner. Learners should be able to explain the reasoning behind their scoring. The instructor should only act as a facilitator and induce open class discussion.

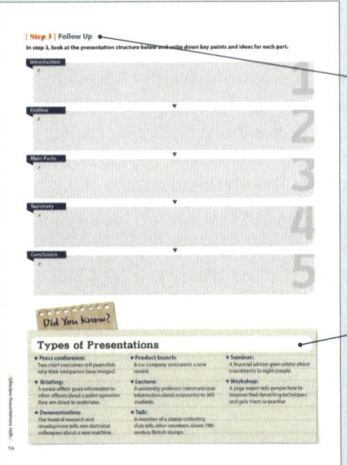

Section 9 — Building Up Presentation-3 Steps

① Step 1: Prep-stage   ② Step 2: The Cases   ③ **Step 3: Follow-Up**

• **Step 3: Follow-Up**
In this section, learners break down and analyze what makes a good case presentation. The structure of the follow-up section differ for each unit, but the idea is to think, write down and share points that makes an effective presentation. There are no right or wrong answers, so the instructor should facilitate the class for an open discussion. This section will act as a guide for making their presentation in the next part "Presentation on Stage".

Section 10 — Did You Know?

In this part of the book, learners will gain useful information which they can utilize in actual presentations. It provides wide-spectrum practical and theoretical information that can be used in different presentation situations. The instructor can use this part as a side reading to take a small break away from the unit. This part should not be heavily focused on since it is only additional information, not must-know information for the unit.

Section 11 Review

All 12 units have a review section which allows learners to recall and review what they have learned throughout the unit. The review section is composed of 3 parts: The first 2 questions are a comprehension check of the unit (theoretical background, presentation tips, language focus) and the last part is dictation. Learners will listen to the good case presentation MP3 and fill in the blanks in the script as they listen. If there is no MP3 player available, the instructor can read the script to the class. It is recommended that learners check their answers with their partners first then go over them together as a whole class.

Section 12 Presentation On Stage

Presentation On Stage is the main activity part of the book and is designed to motivate learners for day to day presentation practice and to help them to incorporate everything they have learned in the unit thus far. All 12 units have different presentation topics and situations. Learners are provided with brief background/history/situational information and are asked to make a presentation. As the main part of the lesson instructors should encourage the learners to utilize newly acquired skills in the unit and should give enough time to prepare and to present. Learners are required to prepare and make a presentation as if it is in real-life. Instructors should make sure everyone gets a chance to present.

Section 13 Checklist

Learners should use this checklist as they are preparing their presentations. The checklist will act as a reminder and as a guide for making effective presentations. The instructor should go over the checklist with the class and encourage students to utilize it. Using the checklist will result in higher presentation score, which learners will evaluate in the next section.

Section 14 Evaluate Yourself & Others

At the end of each presentation, learners will have an opportunity to evaluate self and others on presentation performance. The evaluation is based on whether the learners incorporate all the skills learned and acquired in the unit. This part will allow learners to compare their own presentations with others. The instructor should go over the evaluation rubric and can ask learners to share their scores. The purpose of this section does not lie in scoring itself, but rather help learners to find their strengths and weak spots in making presentations.

Section 15 Let's Recap

This section is for reviewing the "Phrase Bank" expressions. The instructor should recall the phrase bank expressions and check to see if the learners have used them in their presentations. The boxes next to the expressions are placed so that learners can check off the expressions if they have used them. The goal is for learners to check off at least one or two expressions per each category.

Section 16 The Golden Rules

This section provides essential summaries and guidelines for a powerful presentation. Good presentation tips motivate students to instantly build self confidence. Each units provide different tips and general rules for making effective presentations. The tips and rules do not necessarily correspond to the unit's theme but can be applied to all types of presentations in general. The instructor should go over the tips with the class and ask the learners to add several tips of their own. Learners can share additional tips or the class can brainstorm additional tips together.

• **Thinking it Over**

This section is for reviewing the Hints & Tips section. It asks 2 open-ended questions related to the tips above. These questions usually inquire learner's additional ideas and thoughts about the tips and ask for learner's personal experience about giving presentations. The instructor can make this section a discussion based class, but should not focus heavily on it. Hints & Tips are simply additional information that learners should keep in mind when giving presentations.

CONTENTS

Title	Objectives	Case Study	Golden Rules	Page
Unit 1 **Paving the Way for Presentation**	· Describe various kinds of presentations · Explain the basic principles of presentation · Identify what makes a presentation effective	Restoring Company Image	The Basic Must-Know PT Process	11
Unit 2 **Understanding Your Audience**	· Analyze and understand your audience · How to adjust your presentation accordingly · Execute effective presentation logistics · Effectively prepare your presentation in various unexpected situations	Getting Customers' Attention for Feedback	How to Grab the Audience's Attention	21
Unit 3 **Let's Get Started!**	· Understand the importance of making introductions · Prepare an effective introduction · Start a presentation with a strong beginning	Introducing a Product to Gain Appeal	The Triangle of Terror	31
Unit 4 **Linking the Parts**	· Effectively organize a presentation · Arrange your ideas and information for presentation · Determine how to present the material to your audience	Convincing the Town of Calhoun	The Basics: Effective Presentation Organization	41
Unit 5 **A Picture is Worth A 1000 Words**	· Utilize visual material · Effectively deliver the visual materials · Give a presentation using minimal words	Presenting a Revolutionary Device	Utilizing Images to its Fullest Potential	51
Unit 6 **Powerful Delivery**	· Use body language for effective presentations · Have control of yourself to give presentations successfully · Look confident using appropriate presentation skills	Budget cuts, but how?	Tips for Effective Body Language on Stage	61

Title	Objectives	Case Study	Golden Rules	Page
Unit 7 **Adding a Special Touch**	· Deliver audience friendly presentations · Spice up speeches or presentations using a good sense of humor	New Product Launch	Tips for Engaging your Audience	71
Unit 8 **Finishing Strongly**	· Summarize the main concepts effectively at the end of a presentation · Call attention to the closing of a presentation · Help the audience remember the last few seconds of a presentation	End Your Presentation With a Bang	6 Ways to Close Your Presentation	81
Unit 9 **Opening the Floor**	· Deal with questions effectively · Keep credibility established during a presentation · Anticipate unexpected questions	How to Handle Questions	5 Tips to Set the Stage for a Smooth, Yet Captivating Q&A Session	91
Unit 10 **Informative Presentations**	· Give an informative presentation effectively · Guarantee reliable delivery of messages · Build and maintain credibility throughout a presentation	Social Networking Website and How They Work	Types of Informative Presentations	101
Unit 11 **Persuasive Presentations**	· Understand the audience's perception of the topic or subject · Shape your information to specifically address the audience's needs · Convince the audience to agree with an idea or opinion	Confident Delivery: Emotional Appeal	Types of Persuasive Presentations	111
Unit 12 **Refine & Rehearse**	· Make your rehearsal more productive · Use rehearsal time more efficiently · Rehearse to master stage presence	Boost Overall Presentation Quality	What to focus on when Rehearsing a Presentation	121

Getting Started

What are your greatest fears or concerns when it comes to giving presentations?
Let's brainstorm using a mind map.

Making mistakes in front of people

Presentation
My greatest concerns and fears are...

After studying the book:
When you finish studying this book, refer back to this mind map to see how many of your fears you've overcome.

Paving the Way for Presentation

In Unit 1, you will learn how to…
- describe various kinds of presentations
- explain the basic principles of presentation
- identify what makes a presentation effective

Getting Started

Jamie is reading something interesting in the newspaper. What do you think she saw? How does she feel? Share your thoughts and present for at least 1 minute.

Warm-up Questions

1. What is the dividing line between effective and ineffective presentations?

2. What characteristics does a person with good presentation skills have?

Unit 01

Paving the Way for Presentation

1. FYI: Background Knowledge

3 Key Factors for Making Effective Presentations

Power

Effective presentations have enormous power. Famous speeches—such as President Abraham Lincoln's Gettysburg Address, Martin Luther King Jr.'s I Have a Dream—have literally **shaped the world** we live in. The best presentations can delight us, inspire us, and even make us cry. **Responsible** speakers **employ this power to** make the world a better place. **Unethical** speakers have used the same power to bring tyranny and death to millions.

Consequences

Presentations have consequences. When you deliver a dazzling presentation, you enhance your **credibility** and influence the lives of others. Most famous leaders—be they in business, religion, or government—have the ability to present ideas clearly and **persuasively**. Exceptional people who are not famous—**distinguished** teachers, doctors, and community leaders—also understand that presentation speaking skills are **essential** for success.

Inspire

Effective presentation skills can **be demonstrated by** the difference between knowing something and being able **to deliver** it. Effective speaking can mean the difference between having a good idea and knowing how to share it with others. The ability to prepare and deliver a successful presentation is **illustrated by** the difference between interesting audience members and inspiring them to action.

Practice. Let's recap background knowledge.

1 Make a sentence using the chunks from the article above.
 a) shaped the world: _____
 b) employ this power to: _____
 c) be demonstrated by: _____

2 Match the words with their correct meanings.

Credibility • • a) able to cause people to do or believe something
Persuasively • • b) very important and necessary
Distinguished • • c) the quality of being believable or worthy of trust
Essential • • d) known by many people because of some quality or achievement

3 Fill in the blanks with appropriate words from the article above.
 a) _____ speakers employ power of presentation to make the world a better place while _____ speakers have used the same power to bring tyranny and death to millions.
 b) Most famous leaders and great people understand that presentation skills are _____ for success and have the ability to present ideas clearly and _____.
 c) Effective presenters and speakers have to know how to explain the content, how _____ good ideas with others, and _____ the audience into action.

2. Language Focus

Useful Words & Expressions

Below are expressions and phrases that will help you construct effective presentations. Let's review these useful expressions before we dive into the main part of the class.

Chronological Expressions

Ordering	Past	Present
◆ First of all	◆ Last month/year	◆ Currently
◆ Second of all	◆ In the past	◆ Now/Nowadays
◆ Finally	◆ Back in 1997	◆ At present
◆ For my first point	◆ Historically	◆ At the moment
◆ In conclusion	◆ In the last decade	◆ At the present time
◆ For my last part	◆ In the 20th century	

Practice. Write a sentence using one of the expressions from each category.

1) Ordering Category
   e.g.) For my first point, I want to talk about the company's overview.
   » Sentence: _____

2) Past Category
   e.g.) In the past, my company only had 20 employees.
   » Sentence: _____

2) Present Category
   e.g.) My department is hiring new workers at the moment.
   » Sentence: _____

Listed below are useful phrases for starting a presentation. Try to use as many of them as possible during your presentation practices.

Phrase Bank

Welcoming the audience
- Hello, ladies and gentlemen.
- Good afternoon, esteemed guests.
- Good evening, members of the board / fellow colleagues.
- It's my pleasure to welcome you today.

Introducing yourself
- Let me introduce myself.
- I'd like to start by introducing myself. My name is ….
- I am X from Y. I am the manager of…
- My name is …. I would like to talk to you today about …

Introducing your subject
- Today I'm going to talk about…
- The subject of my presentation is …
- The theme of my talk is …
- I'm here today to present…
- I'll be talking about…

To get the audience's attention
- Have you ever heard of …?
- Every day you encounter …
- Today's topic is of particular interest to those of you / us who…
- My topic is / will be very important for you because…
- You may have wondered …

3. 3 Steps Building Up

Case Study: Restoring Company Image

| Step 1 | Prep-Stage

Read the case study context and the situation. Answer the comprehension questions and brainstorm presentation ideas.

The Context			Real Situation
The Company	**The Presenter**	**The Audience**	**The Presentation**
H Motors, was one of the leading automobile companies, but over the last few years, its image has become negative and weak. It has recently created the post of PR Manager in order to improve the company's image in the market.	Jay Smith is H Motors' new PR manager. One of the first things he did was to organize a meeting to discuss its corporate image. In particular, how to restore a positive corporate image.	Jay Smith invited the senior managers of the company and outside consultants. They are expecting to participate in a meeting about the corporate image of H Motors.	Unfortunately, Jay gets the date wrong. He realizes his mistake only when his secretary tells him that the audience is waiting in the conference room. He starts the meeting with a short presentation. The presentation should introduce the main topics for discussion.

1. **Imagine you are in the audience. What kind of presentation would you expect from Jay Smith? What are some things you would want to hear from him?**

    ✎

    ✎

    ✎

    ✎

2. **If you were Jay Smith, the presenter, which one of the 3 key presentation concepts (power, consequences, inspire) would you focus on the most / the least?**

    * To recall information, please refer to the background knowledge section on the book.

    ✎

    ✎

    ✎

    ✎

Step 2 | Case Comparison

Read the two case presentations and determine which one is more effective.

Case 1

I am very sorry that **I am late.** I was so busy with my other work that **I completely forgot** about the meeting that I scheduled today. So how has everyone's day been so far? Well, let's get going then. So I invited everyone here today because I wanted to discuss something of importance. So the main issue here is that the corporate image of our company, H Motors, has been going downhill for quite some time. **I called all of you to brainstorm ideas** that can improve our company's image. So do any of you have some **ideas to start us off?** Anything will be appreciated.

Case 2

Thank you for waiting patiently. I am Jay Smith and I was **recently hired** as the PR manager to **resolve** an important issue. Before we get started, **I have invited here** today the senior managers of our company Mr. Jackson and Mrs. William. I've also invited expert consultants Mr. Kim and Ms. Black. The issue we are facing is the fact that the corporate image of our company, H Motors has been **recently declining.** With the **growing popularity** of 'Go Green' movements, this social change has become **a niche for** many different companies, including some in the automobile industries. Our company is **lagging behind,** I would like to consult the experts and **ask for advice** from the experienced seniors here with us today.

1. Based on the rubric criteria, score the two cases and add up the total score.

Type	Unsatisfactory	Poor	Fair/Average	Good	Excellent
Score	1	2	3	4	5
Tempo	☐	☐	☐	☐	☐
Volume	☐	☐	☐	☐	☐
Expression	☐	☐	☐	☐	☐
Articulation	☐	☐	☐	☐	☐
Sentence length	☐	☐	☐	☐	☐
Register / Style	☐	☐	☐	☐	☐
Linkers	☐	☐	☐	☐	☐
Emphasizers / Minimizers	☐	☐	☐	☐	☐

» Case 1 Total Score :

» Case 2 Total Score :

2. Which presentation case do you think is better? Support your opinion and discuss it with your partner.

| **Step 3** | **Follow Up**

Look at the presentation structure below and write down key points and ideas for each part.

Introduction

▼

Outline

▼

Main Parts

▼

Summary

▼

Conclusion

Types of Presentations

- **Press conference:**
  Two chief executives tell journalists why their companies have merged.

- **Briefing:**
  A senior officer gives information to other officers about a police operation they are about to undertake.

- **Demonstration:**
  The head of research and development demonstrates non-technical colleagues about a new machine.

- **Product launch:**
  A car company announces a new model.

- **Lecture:**
  A university professor communicates information about economics to 300 students.

- **Talk:**
  A member of a stamp-collecting club tells other members about 19th century British stamps.

- **Seminar:**
  A financial adviser gives advice about investments to eight people.

- **Workshop:**
  A yoga expert tells people how to improve their breathing techniques and gets them to practice.

Review

1. **The sentences below provide examples of expressions people might use in certain presentations. Match each example to the appropriate presentation type.**

a	demonstration	a — As you can see, this prototype is far in compare to we've done before.
b	talk	b — I'm going to give each group a series of problems faced by an imaginary company, and I want you to suggest possible solutions.
c	product launch	c — The parachutists will come in at 08:30 and land in two waves, here and there.
d	workshop	d — The X300 has the most advanced features of any car in its class.

2. **Place the right expressions according to its category.**

   a) Good evening, members of the board/ fellow colleagues.
   b) The theme of my talk is
   c) It's a pleasure to welcome you today.
   d) You may have wondered …
   e) Every day you encounter …
   f) Today I'm going to talk about…

   ✓ Welcoming the audience   ✓ Introducing your subject   ✓ To get the audience's attention
   _____ , _____   _____ , _____   _____ , _____

3. **For additional listening practice, you may listen to good case mp3 or read the script below and complete the sentences.**

   Thank you for waiting patiently. I am Jay Smith and I was ⓐ _____ as the PR manager ⓑ _____ an important issue. Before we get started, ⓒ _____ here today the senior managers of our company Mr. Jackson and Mrs. William. I've also invited expert consultants Mr. Kim and Ms. Black. The issue that our company, H Motors, is facing is the fact that the corporate image of our company has been ⓓ _____. With the ⓔ _____ of 'Go Green' movements, this social change has become ⓕ _____ many different companies including automobile industries. With our company ⓖ _____, I would like to consult the experts and ⓗ _____ from the experienced seniors here with us today.

   Answer Key : ⓐ recently hired ⓑ to resolve ⓒ I have invited ⓓ recently declining ⓔ growing popularity ⓕ a niche for ⓖ lagging behind ⓗ ask for advice

"Remember, the more presentations you listen to, the better presenter you will become."

Presentation On Stage

Step 1 | **Presentation Practice**

First read the information below about the history of Apple Inc.
Then create a presentation slide and a script to go with it. Finally, present to the class!

Apple Inc.

History

1977	○	Founded by Steve Jobs, Steve Wozniak, Ronald Wayne
1984	•	The Apple Macintosh is released
1989	•	Mac Portable is released
2001	•	Apple iPod is released
2003	•	iTunes music store opens
2007	•	iPhone is released
2010	•	Tablet computing develops with the iPad

Based on the information above, create a 1-pg presentation slide.

» **Presentation Slide**

Based on what you wrote in the presentation slide, write a script to go with it.

» **Presentation Script**

✓ Checklist

Use the checklist to prepare an effective presentation.

☐ Why are you speaking? (Purpose)

☐ Who is in your audience? (Audience)

☐ Are you believable? (Credibility)

☐ Where and when will you speak? (Logistics)

☐ What ideas and information should you include? (Content)

☐ How should you arrange your content? (Organization)

☐ How should you deliver your presentation?(Performance)

Step 2 | Evaluate Yourself & Others

Mark △ for yourself and mark ○ to evaluate others.

Evaluating Presentation Performance

Objectives	1	2	3	4	5
· clearly stated					
· appropriate for audience/subject					

Content	1	2	3	4	5
· well researched					
· broad / detailed enough					
· content relevant					
· appropriate for the audience					

Organization	1	2	3	4	5
· carefully planned					
· coherent					
· clear					
· well-timed					

Visual Aids	1	2	3	4	5
· appropriate for subject and audience					
· clearly legible and structured					
· introduced and explained well					
· support overall message					

Delivery	1	2	3	4	5
· rate of speech and quality					
· established audience rapport					
· eye contact					
· appear confident and positive					
· use body language					
· clearly audible					

Language	1	2	3	4	5
· clear					
· accurate					
· appropriate					
· well-pronounced					
· used signaling phrases					

Overall	1	2	3	4	5
· message clear					
· objective achieved					
· interesting					
· enjoyable and interesting					
· informative					
· motivating					

» Your Score: _____

» Others: _____

Let's Recap!

Check to see if you have used any of the phrases from the Phrase Bank.

*Remember! Using these phrases will help you deliver a more effective presentation.

◆ **Welcoming the audience**
- ☐ Hello, ladies and gentlemen.
- ☐ Good afternoon, esteemed guests.
- ☐ Good evening, members of the board / fellow colleagues.
- ☐ It's a pleasure to welcome you today.

◆ **Introducing yourself**
- ☐ Let me introduce myself.
- ☐ I'd like to start by introducing myself. My name is….
- ☐ I am X from Y. I am the manager of…
- ☐ My name is …. I would like to talk to you today about …

◆ **Introducing your subject**
- ☐ Today I'm going to talk about…
- ☐ The subject of my presentation is …
- ☐ The theme of my talk is …
- ☐ I'm here today to present…
- ☐ I'll be talking about…

◆ **To get the audience's attention**
- ☐ Have you ever heard of …?
- ☐ Every day you encounter …
- ☐ Today's topic is of particular interest to those of you / us who…
- ☐ My topic is / will be very important for you because…
- ☐ You may have wondered …

The Golden Rules for Unit 1

The Basic Must-Know PT Process

1. Leave nothing to chance
2. Have a strong start
3. Be concise
4. Talk to your audience
5. Know your audience
6. Speak naturally and be yourself
7. Treat your audience as equals
8. Take your time
9. Choose effective visuals
10. Enjoy the experience
11. Welcome questions
12. Finish strongly
13. Develop your own style

Thinking it Over

1. Which of these tips do you find most useful? Can you add any other tips?

2. Have you ever presented to a foreigner? How different were the audience from those in your own country?

Understanding Your Audience

In Unit 2, you learn how to...
- analyze and understand your audience
- adjust your presentation accordingly
- execute effective presentation logistics
- effectively prepare your presentation in various unexpected situations

Getting Started
Derick seems upset and frustrated. What do you think happened to him 5 minutes ago? What do you think will happen after 5 minutes? Make a story and present for at least 1 minute.

Warm-up Questions
1. How can knowing your audiences help you to present better?

2. Have you ever encountered any presentation logistics problems before?

Unit 02

Understanding Your Audience

1. FYI: Background Knowledge

Why do you need to understand your audience?

Audiences and Logistics

Audience-Focused Communication

Being a truly effective speaker requires understanding, respecting, and adapting to the people who will be listening to you. Understanding and adapting to your audience **has several practical advantages.** A **thorough understanding** of your audience can help you focus your presentation and decide how to narrow your topic. An audience-focused approach can simplify and shorten your preparation time by using the audience as a **criterion for deciding** what to include or exclude. For example, if your audience is the general public, **jargon** will be difficult for them to understand thus thorough explanations will be necessary. On the other hand, if your audience consists of professionals, you will want to **get straight to the point.**

Logistics

Being able to adapt to the location where you will be presenting requires **critical thinking about logistics.** The term **logistics** describes the strategic planning, arranging, and use of people, facilities, time and materials **relevant** to your presentation. There are four main logistics questions you should ask yourself when you are planning. They are: who, where, when and how. These four **interrogatives** refer to people, location, time, and materials, respectively. Understanding your audience (who), identifying the setting/facility in which you will be presenting (where), mastering over the allotted time (when), and making decisions on the best methods of **relaying your message to** the audience (how) are all important assets of planning appropriate logistics for your presentation.

Practice. Let's recap background knowledge.

1 Fill in the blanks using the bolded words and expressions from the background knowledge article.

   a) Don't beat around the bush when talking to professionals, just _____

   b) Familiarizing yourself with the location of your presentation requires _____

   c) Difficult and technical terms used in various professions are known as _____

   d) Who, where, when, and how are the four main _____ of logistics.

   e) Analyzing and adjusting to your audience _____ such as creating more compact but more effective presentations.

2 Match the words with their correct meanings.

   Who   •   • a) the location at which the presentation is going to take place
   Where   •   • b) planning various methods you are going to use in the presentation
   When   •   • c) managing time such as time given for your presentation, etc
   How   •   • d) audience size, age group, ethnicity, etc

3 Choose true (T) or false (F).

   a) Knowing your audience will only hinder your ability to get the point across because you may exclude some important information. _____

   b) Having good logistics will only improve the way the audience sees you during your presentation. _____

   c) It is better to simplify jargon and provide background knowledge if the audience members are not familiar with the topic you are presenting. _____

2. Language Focus

Phrase Bank

Listed below are useful expressions for gaining the audience's attention throughout the presentation. Try to use them during your presentation practices.

Giving an example
- Now let's take an example. An example of this can be found…
- To illustrate this…
- Let's see this through an example.
- For example / for instance…
- A good example of this is…

To rephrase
- Let me rephrase that…
- In other words…
- Another way of saying the same thing is…
- That is to say…

Introducing your subject
- Today I'm going to talk about…
- The subject of my presentation is…
- The theme of my talk is…
- I'm here today to present…
- I'll be talking about…

To emphasize
- I'd like to emphasize the fact that/to stress / to highlight / to underline…
- What I tried to bring out is…
- What we need to focus on is…
- The important thing to remember is…
- We did see a noticeable difference.
- What I'd like to show today is the difference between the two products.

To refer to common knowledge
- As you all may well know…
- It is generally accepted that…
- As you are probably aware…

To refer to what an expert says
- I quote the words of…
- In the words of…
- According to…

Useful Words & Expressions

- Below are expressions and phrases that will help you construct effective presentations.
- Review the expressions and try to use them in the presentation practice section.

Emphasizing Interjections

- **in detail**
  Now let me explain this theory in detail.

- **notably**
  Most notably, Samsung has been winning the patent war against Apple.

- **keep in mind**
  Please keep in mind the previous figure as we continue.

- **to summarize**
  To summarize this graph, the sales points in the latter half are strongly correlated.

- **draw your attention to**
  I would like to draw your attention to the latest figure.

- **what you can see here**
  What you can see here on this graph is a linear trend.

- **what do you think**
  What do you think is the reason behind the recent declines?

- **if you guessed**
  If you guessed "'no'" then you are indeed correct.

- **what we need to focus on**
  What we need to focus on is the current global trends in IT.

- **to emphasize**
  I would like to emphasize this graph here.

- **to stress**
  In order to stress this factor, I made a visual aid.

- **to highlight**
  I would like to highlight this important fact.

1 Fill in the blanks using the most appropriate emphasizing interjections.

| notably | keep in mind |
| what do you think | in detail |

a) The advancement of computer technology has been exponential since the past decade. _____, Bill Gates and Steve Jobs have played a significant role in this progress.

b) Please make sure to _____ that what you see isn't all there is.

c) Could you please explain this concept to me _____?

d) _____ will happen when the demand increases while supply decreases?

3. 3 Steps Building Up

Case Study: Getting Customers' Attention for Feedback

| Step 1 | Prep-Stage

Read the case study context and the situation. Answer the comprehension questions and brainstorm presentation ideas.

The Context			Real Situation
The Company	**The Presenter**	**The Audience**	**The Presentation**
The company, J Telecom, has recently released new smart phones. However, due to the rapidly growing smart phone market, they wanted to get some information from young customers.	The CEO of the company, Tim Richards, decided to personally meet with the young customers to show them the company's new phone as well as to hear the customers' opinions and feedback.	Tim decided to give a short presentation to the students at the University of California to show them the company's new smart phones as well as to get feedback and ideas on what the customers want.	Due to the students' busy schedules, Tim has to choose the right time as well as the size of the audience he wants to get feedback from so that he can either book a large seminar room or a small group room. He also needs to start his presentation well to grab their attention.

1. What are some different ways to approach different audiences? (young audience, highly educated audience, elderly, etc)

    ✎

    ✎

    ✎

    ✎

2. Imagine you are Tim Richards, about to give the presentation. Decide how you would approach the students at University of California.

    a) What audience size would you want?
    b) How will you catch their attention?

    ✎

    ✎

    ✎

    ✎

Step 2 | Case Comparison

Read the two case presentations and determine which one is more effective.

🎧 Case 1

Tim took a look at the overall students' schedules and found that many students have one or two hours free during lunch time. So he decided to book the auditorium with a built-in projector so that he could invite approximately 100 students. He also let the students know in advance that he would be giving a short presentation with free lunch. Additionally, he decided to provide the attendees with Bluetooth clickers so that the audience can do the survey remotely. Prior to the presentation, he checked to see if everything is working perfectly. Over 100 students showed up. Tim began his presentation by saying, "Good afternoon everyone. My name is Tim Richards and I am the CEO of J Telecom. Thank you for coming today and please keep in mind that your opinions are my command!"

Case 2 🎧

Tim decided to personally meet with the students to get their opinion. He created a booth in front of the student community center. He printed his survey to get information from students as well as their opinions on today's smart phones. Unfortunately, due to the students' busy schedules, the majority of them just passed by the booth without giving Tim any attention. Also, due to the time it took to read and complete the survey, many students rejected the survey and left. By the end of the day, he was left with a few completed surveys and only two dozen of the students took a brief look at his company's new smart phones.

1. Based on the rubric criteria, score the two cases and add up the total score.

Type / Score	Unsatisfactory / 1	Poor / 2	Fair/Average / 3	Good / 4	Excellent / 5
Time management for presenter	☐	☐	☐	☐	☐
Time management for audience	☐	☐	☐	☐	☐
Provided refreshment	☐	☐	☐	☐	☐
Scheduled the room	☐	☐	☐	☐	☐
Inspected the room prior to presentation	☐	☐	☐	☐	☐
Organization of media equipment	☐	☐	☐	☐	☐

» **Case 1 Total Score** :

» **Case 2 Total Score** :

2. Which presentation case do you think is better? Support your opinion and discuss it with your partner.

| Step 3 | Follow Up

Look at the 4 logistics below and write down the key points for each.

Who

1

Where

2

When

3

How

4

Did You Know?

Audience Size and Presentation

Audience size affects how you will present a topic and how you will target it to a specific audience. Here are the terms.

- ◆ **Small Group Facilitation Skills**
  - Audience-centered
  - Hand-written overheads
  - Customer-relevant visuals

- ◆ **Interactive Training Skills**
  - Content-centered
  - Unlimited overheads
  - Content-specific visuals

- ◆ **Structured Group Dynamic Skills**
  - Content/speaker-centered
  - Targeted overheads
  - Application visuals

- ◆ **Big Room Presentation Skills**
  - Speaker-centered
  - Limited overheads
  - Simple visuals

Review

1. **Audiences & Logistics: Rearrange the words to create a sentence.**

   a) has / advantages / Understanding / practical / and adapting / to your audience / several.

   ....

   ....

   b) narrow your topic. / your presentation / your audience / focus / and decide how to / understanding of / can help you / A thorough

   ....

   ....

   c) where you will be / logistics. / Adapting to / critical thinking / the place / speaking / about / requires

   ....

   ....

2. **Connect the expressions according to its category.**

Big Room Presentation Skills	○		○	a) Customer-relevant visuals
Structured Group Dynamic Skills	○		○	b) Simple visuals
Interactive Training Skills	○		○	c) Speaker centered
Small Group Facilitation Skills	○		○	d) Content-specific visuals
			○	e) Audience centered
			○	f) Content/speaker centered
			○	g) Application visuals
			○	h) Content centered

3. **Read each statement and list them in the order of audience size. The biggest group will be (1) while smallest will be (3).**

    It requires a speaker focused presentation. It is best to arrive prior to the presentation to check to see if there will be a working microphone so that everyone can hear you.

    This size of audience is easy to manage. You can get personal with these individuals and names are necessary. Usually these types of presentations are audience-focused.

    These types of presentations require a fine balance between the content and the audience. This size of audience is manageable and allows room for some interaction.

Presentation On Stage

Step 1 — **Plan a presentation**

You are the marketing manager, and you have recently received a script of a movie. You now have to plan, prepare, and introduce the script to one of the given audiences. Please prepare the presentation in groups.

◎ Audiences

Film distributer/financial entity
(5 people, available during the mornings, major corporation)

Director
(1 person, available during evenings, well known director)

Actors and supporting casts
(30 people Available during noon, rising stars)

◎ Movie Summary

The movie is about lovers who meet on a cruise ship. However, soon after their encounter, the ship sinks and the lovers need to fight for their lives to escape the gradually sinking cruise ship. In the end, only one survives.

◎ Method of Approach

- The film distributer is not interested in the movie but in who will be casted for the movie because that determines the popularity of the movie.
- The director is interested in the overall story of the movie. Does it have a twist? Will it make the audience emotional?
- The actors and supporting casts are interested in a little bit of the story but majorly on who will be directing the movie.

» **Write down one key point you want to deliver for each of the target audience.**

- Film distributer
- Director
- Actors/supporting casts

✓ Logistics Checklist

☐ Choose a time that is convenient for the presenter and audience   ☐ Inspect the room prior to presentation

☐ Provide refreshments and/or lunch.   ☐ Arrange for the media equipment

☐ Schedule the room

Step 2 | Evaluate Yourself & Others

Mark △ for yourself and mark ○ to evaluate others.

Evaluating Presentation Performance

Audience	1	2	3	4	5
· Did you use visual aids to grab the attention of the audience					
· Was the subject appropriate for the audience					
· Were you straight to the point					

Who	1	2	3	4	5
· Did you capture the right audience					
· Was the audience size well-planned					

When	1	2	3	4	5
· Was the presentation time convenient for you					
· Was the presentation time convenient for the audience					
· How long was the presentation					
· Did you use appropriate emphasizers					
· Do you think the audiences were interested					

Where	1	2	3	4	5
· Was the room big enough to fit the size of your audience					
· Did you check the room to see if the media equipment would be useable					

How	1	2	3	4	5
· Did you use the right equipment to relay your message					
· Was it good enough to grab the audience's attention					
· Did you provide refreshments					
· Did you arrange for media equipment					

Emphasizers	1	2	3	4	5
· Were you loud and clear to keep the audience focused					

» Your Score: _____   » Others: _____

Let's Recap!

Check to see if you have used any of the phrases from the Phrase Bank.

*Remember! Using these phrases will help you deliver a more effective presentation.

◆ **Giving an example**
- ☐ Now let's take an example. An example of this can be found…
- ☐ To illustrate this…
- ☐ Let's see this through an example.
- ☐ For example / for instance…
- ☐ A good example of this is…

◆ **To emphasize**
- ☐ I'd like to emphasize the fact that/to stress / to highlight / to underline…
- ☐ What I tried to bring out is…
- ☐ What we need to focus on is…
- ☐ The important thing to remember is…
- ☐ We did see a noticeable difference.
- ☐ What I'd like to show today is the difference between the two products.

◆ **To rephrase**
- ☐ Let me rephrase that…
- ☐ In other words…
- ☐ Another way of saying the same thing is…
- ☐ That is to say…

◆ **To refer to common knowledge**
- ☐ As you all may well know…
- ☐ It is generally accepted that…
- ☐ As you are probably aware…

◆ **To refer to what an expert says**
- ☐ I quote the words of…
- ☐ In the words of…
- ☐ According to…

The Golden Rules for Unit 2

How to Grab the Audience's Attention

1. Know who your audience is
2. Relate to the audience with a story that complements the subject
3. Open strong with interesting facts or problems relating to your topic
4. Guide your audience's eyes to where you want them to be
5. Share quotes from a famous individual or use analogies
6. Get the audience involved
7. Ask rhetorical questions or thought-provoking-questions
8. Ask a 'show-of-hands' question
9. Don't be vague. Be precise and show them facts.
10. Be concise with your slides
11. Keep the audience guessing as if they are assembling a puzzle with the information that you provide
12. End great
13. Don't underestimate the audience.
14. Be confident! You are the professional on the subject!

Thinking it Over

1. Rather than using just words, what alternative methods can be used to draw the audience's attention?
2. Have you ever talked about a topic, on which you're an expert, with someone who isn't? If so, was it difficult to explain yourself?

Let's Get Started

In Unit 3, you will learn how to…
- understand the importance of making introductions
- prepare an effective introduction
- start a presentation with a strong beginning

Getting Started

James is getting into trouble with his boss. What do you think the boss is saying? Make a story and present for at least 1 minute.

Warm-up Questions

1. Public speaking ranks as the number one fear for Americans. What makes you nervous about public speaking? What do you fear about presenting in front of people?

2. What do you think are the three key factors that must be included in an effective introduction?

Unit 03

Let's Get Started

1. FYI: Background Information

Having a Strong Start for your Presentation

Introduction

Introductions as Mini-presentations

The importance of the introduction to your presentation warrants as much attention as the actual presentation itself. Just like the idiom 'First impressions are the most lasting' with a great start, you can create a positive, lasting impression and pave the way for a presentation that achieves your purpose. Psychologists have reported that we recall items that are presented first. This phenomenon is known as the **'primary effect.'** Thus, the beginning of the presentation is the point at which the audiences' attention to new stimuli is **at its peak**. Therefore it is crucial to capitalize on this effect by having a striking introduction.

To prepare for an effective introduction, you must first understand what it can and should accomplish. While the purpose of the introduction is to **introduce your topic to your audience**, it also introduces the audience to you. The introduction gives the audience time to adjust, settle in, block out distractions, and **focus their attention on** you and your message. It simultaneously gives you, as the presenter, the chance to familiarize yourself with the audience, relax, and make any **last-minute adjustments** to what you want to say and how you want to say it. A good introduction establishes a relationship among **three elements: you, your message and your audience.**

Practice. Let's recap background knowledge

1 Fill in the blanks using the bolded words from the background information passage.

a) First impressions are important because we recall items that are presented first. Psychologists have named this the _____.

b) The beginning of the presentation is where the audience's attention is _____.

c) Your introduction gives the _____ time to adjust, settle in, block out distraction, and _____ on you and your message.

d) The introduction _____ helps the presenter to get a chance to get a _____! relax, and make any _____.

2 In pairs, answer the following questions using the above information in pairs.

a) Explain the dual effect of introductions, helping the audience as well as yourself.

b) What does 'primary effect' mean? How does it relate to an introduction?

3 Choose true (T) or false (F).

a) With a positive lasting impression by great introduction, you can obtain the trust of the audience and consequently their attention. _____

b) Primary effect refers to a phenomenon where the audience will remember the last thing mentioned in the presentation. _____

c) The purpose of the introduction is only to get the audience ready for the forthcoming information. _____

d) The beginning of the presentation is the point at which the audience will be open and ready for new information. _____

2. Language Focus

Listed below are useful expressions for guiding the audience throughout the presentation. Try to use them during your presentation practices.

Phrase Bank

The main purpose
- What I would like to do today is to explain / illustrate / give a general overview of / to outline / to have a look at…
- What I want my listeners to get from my speech is …
- I'd like to update you on/inform you about…

Structuring
- I have broken / divided my speech down / up into X parts.
- In the first part I give a few basic definitions. In the next section I will explain.
- In part X, I am going to show… In the last place I would like / want to give a practical example.

Timing
- My presentation will take about 30 minutes.
- It'll take around 15 minutes to cover the main issues.
- This won't take more than…

Handouts
- Does everyone have a handout / copy of the presentation slides? Please take one and pass them on.
- I can email the report to anybody who wants it.
- Don't worry about taking notes.

Questions
- I'd ask you to save your questions for the end.
- There will be plenty of time at the end of my speech for questions and discussion.
- You may interrupt me at any moment to ask questions or make comments.

Useful Words & Expressions

Presentations can be done formally as well as casually. Here are some of more formal and less formal expressions used in an introduction.

More formal expressions used in an introduction	Less formal expressions used in an introduction
• Good afternoon, ladies and gentlemen.	• Hi, everyone.
• Today I would like to …	• In my talk, I'll tell you about …
• Let me start by introducing myself. My name is…	• Today, I'm going to talk about …
• It's a pleasure to welcome you today.	• It's good to see you guys here.
• The topic of today's presentation is …	• What I want to do today is …

1 Choose either more formal (M) or less formal (L).

a) Many of you are aware of the decline in the US economy.

b) So, if you guys have any questions I'd be happy to answer them later.

c) Thanks for coming to this presentation. It won't take long.

d) Good afternoon ladies and gentlemen. It's my pleasure to be here today.

3. 3 Steps Building Up

Case Study: Introducing a Product to Gain Appeal

| Step 1 | Prep-Stage

Read the case study context and the situation. Answer the comprehension questions and brainstorm presentation ideas.

The Context			Real Situation
The Company	**The Presenter**	**The Audience**	**The Presentation**
An independent company, PR Studio has developed innovative security software which can alter the history of personal information protection on computerized electronic software.	Martin Szczyglowski, the head developer of his independent company, has to present the appeal of his software at an international conference so that various software engineering companies will potentially integrate his system in their electronic devices.	The conference has invited many speakers from giants such as S Engineering, J Security Firm and many others to present their software and various electronic devices. The conference is focused on connecting these large companies with smaller ones for new innovative ideas.	Since there are many small independent companies presenting similar ideas, most of the audience is having a hard time remembering who these presenters are. Martin has to give a strong introduction so that he may stand out above all the other small companies.

1. **What are some do's and don'ts for making an effective introduction for your presentation?**

   ✎

   ✎

   ✎

   ✎

2. **Imagine that you are the representative of PR Studio, about to give presentation. Decide on the points of an appealing introduction so that you and your product may stand out from the rest of the presenters.**

   ✎

   ✎

   ✎

   ✎

| Step 2 | Case Comparison

Read the two case presentations and determine which one is more effective.

🎧 Introduction 1

Hi, everyone. My name is **Martin** and I work at PR Studio which is an independent company. **Thanks** for coming today to my panel. **Well,** today I'm going to introduce you **guys** to our new coding method which will allow you to take the security of today's social information to another level. **Okay, so** with the ever-growing brilliant minds of computer technology, so many people are getting their social information exposed to bad people online. **So** we came up with a complex method which can further the complexity of your security codes. **So let's stop beating around the bush** and get straight to the point.

🎧 Introduction 1

Good afternoon everyone. My name is **Martin Szczyglowski** and **it is my pleasure to be speaking here to you today. I am the head developer** of the independent company, PR Studio, and we specialize in the development of security softwares. Today, **my topic of interest** is the innovative coding method of social security programs. With the advancement of computer technology, maintain secure control over your social information is getting difficult by the minute. Therefore, today, **I would like to introduce you** to a new method of Unicoding, **followed by an explanation of** how to implement this method in today's security systems. **Lastly,** I will demonstrate how this method benefits us as a whole. **Let's not keep you waiting and get started. Please, don't hesitate to interrupt me if you have any questions during my presentation.**

1. Based on the rubric criteria, score the two cases and add up the total score.

Type / Score	Unsatisfactory / 1	Poor / 2	Fair/Average / 3	Good / 4	Excellent / 5
Welcome the audience	☐	☐	☐	☐	☐
Introduced himself	☐	☐	☐	☐	☐
Stated topic and title	☐	☐	☐	☐	☐
Explained why topic is important	☐	☐	☐	☐	☐
Outlined structure of the talk	☐	☐	☐	☐	☐
Provided preview of the main point	☐	☐	☐	☐	☐
Motivate listeners to accept main goal	☐	☐	☐	☐	☐
Stated when the questions can be asked	☐	☐	☐	☐	☐

» **Case 1** Total Score :

» **Case 2** Total Score :

2. Which presentation case do you think is better? Support your opinion and discuss it with your partner.

Step 3 | Follow Up

a) Write down key points for good introduction.

....

....

....

b) Based on the case presentation, list how the speaker established a good relationship amongst the three elements of an introduction.

Did You Know?

Introduction length
How long should my introduction be?

Generally, your introduction should take no longer than 10% of your overall presentation time. Although introductions are good, you never want to make your audience drift off from your presentation. There are sometimes exceptions to this rule, where you have a hostile audience or distrustful audience. In this case, you may need a longer introduction to establish common ground where belief, attitude, or experience shared by the speaker and the audience come to an agreement. However, generally, 10% is ample amount of time for achieving this goal.

Review

1. **Effective Introductions: Rearrange the words to create a sentence.**

   ⓐ the introduction / your topic / of / The / is to / your audience./ purpose / to / introduce

   _____

   _____

   ⓑ pave the way / that / your purpose. / for a presentation / and / lasting impression / You / achieves / can create / a positive

   _____

   _____

   ⓒ A / you, / and your audience. / three elements: / establishes / among / your message / introduction / good / a relationship

   _____

   _____

   _____

2. **Connect the expressions according to whether they are necessary or unnecessary in an introduction.**

   Essential element •

   Unnecessary element •

   • **a)** Introduce the audience to you

   • **b)** Jokes to start the presentation

   • **c)** Abbreviation of terms or phrases

   • **d)** The purpose of this presentation.

3. **Fill in the blanks in this introduction passage using the appropriate formal expressions.**

   ✓ ladies and gentlemen
   ✓ let me start by introducing myself.
   ✓ topic of today's presentation
   ✓ welcome you today

   ⓐ Good afternoon _____. It's a pleasure to

   ⓑ _____. I have met some of you, but

   ⓒ _____. My name is Jaime Jones, the Vice president of this company.

   The **ⓓ** _____ is global trends in the IT market.

Presentation On Stage

Step 1 — **Plan a presentation**

You are the recruiting manager and a co-owner of a State Farm car insurance company seeking students at the University of California for an internship position. Introduce yourself and the company to get the pessimistic students interested in the internship position. Please prepare the presentation in groups.

◎ Audiences
Students at the University of California are pessimistic about venturing into the internship position. These students are afraid of trying new things and are indecisive because they worry it might hurt their university life and marks.

◎ The Company and Benefits of the Position
Your company has been looking for young individuals that are willing to get their foot-in-the-door. In order to make this internship more appealing, you made a deal with the school board to make this internship a co-operation placement. As a result, upon students finishing the internship, a 2.5 school credit as well as a job position at the company will be granted.

◎ Brainstorming Ideas:
Discuss the following question with your group first. Then write down key message you want to deliver to the students at the University of California.

1) What are some ways to get student's interest? How can you appeal to them?
2) Imagine that you are one of the students looking for an internship position. What are some things you look for?

» **Key Message for Students:**

✓ Checklist for Effective Introductions

- ☐ Welcome the audience
- ☐ Introduce yourself
- ☐ State the topic and title
- ☐ Explain why the topic is important
- ☐ Outline the structure and time of the talk
- ☐ Provide a preview of the main points
- ☐ Motivate listeners to accept presentation goals
- ☐ State when the audience can ask questions

Step 2: Evaluate Yourself & Others

Mark △ for yourself and mark ○ to evaluate others.

Evaluating Presentation Performance

Introduce yourself	1	2	3	4	5
· Did you introduce yourself to the audience					
· Did you appeal yourself to make the audience trust you and your information					
· Did you make a good impression					

Title or subject	1	2	3	4	5
· Did you introduce your title					
· Was the title catchy					

Purpose	1	2	3	4	5
· Did you provide the audience with the purpose of this presentation					
· Did you relay to the audience why this presentation is important					

Length	1	2	3	4	5
· Did you tell the audience how long your presentation is going to be					
· Was the introduction reasonable in terms of length					

Outline	1	2	3	4	5
· Did you provide the audience with the table of contents					
· Did you give them a preview of what your main points are					
· Did you tell them how the presentation is set up to get the message across					

Questions	1	2	3	4	5
· Did you tell the audience when you will address the questions					

» **Your Score:** _____   » **Others:** _____

Let's Recap!

Check to see if you have used any of the phrases from the Phrase Bank.

*Remember! Using these phrases will help you deliver a more effective presentation.

◆ **The main purpose**
- ☐ What I would like to do today is to explain / illustrate / give a general overview of/to outline / to have a look at…
- ☐ What I want my listeners to get out of my speech is …
- ☐ I'd like to update you on / inform you about…

◆ **Structuring**
- ☐ I have broken / divided my speech down / up into X parts.
- ☐ In the first part I give a few basic definitions. In the next section I will explain.
- ☐ In part X, I am going to show… In the last place I would like / want to give a practical example.

◆ **Timing**
- ☐ My presentation will take about 30 minutes.
- ☐ It'll take around 15 minutes to cover the main issues.
- ☐ This won't take more than…

◆ **Handouts**
- ☐ Does everyone have a handout / copy of the presentation slides? Please take one and pass them on.
- ☐ I can email the report to anybody who wants it.
- ☐ Don't worry about taking notes.

◆ **Questions**
- ☐ I'd ask you to save your questions for the end.
- ☐ There will be plenty of time at the end of my speech for questions and discussion.
- ☐ You may interrupt me at any moment to ask questions or make comments.

The Golden Rules for Unit 3

The Triangle of Terror

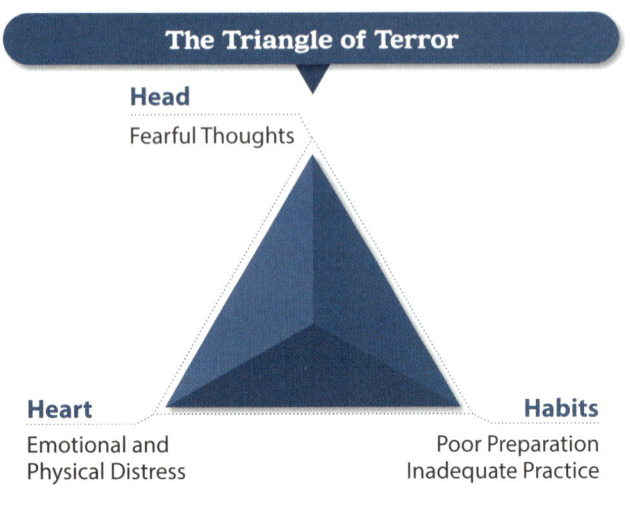

The Triangle of Terror
- Head: Fearful Thoughts
- Heart: Emotional and Physical Distress
- Habits: Poor Preparation, Inadequate Practice

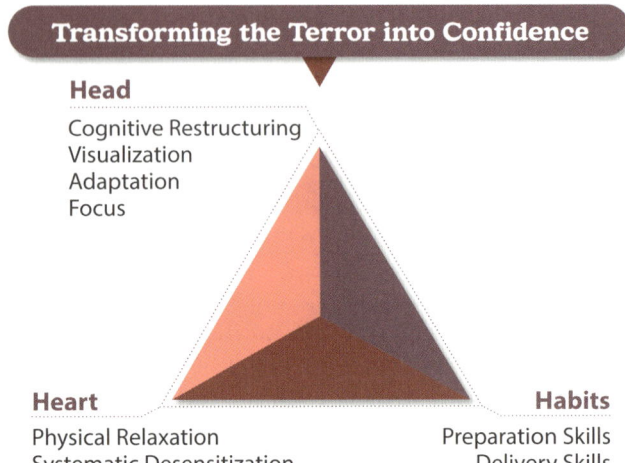

Transforming the Terror into Confidence
- Head: Cognitive Restructuring, Visualization, Adaptation, Focus
- Heart: Physical Relaxation, Systematic Desensitization, Share Your Fears
- Habits: Preparation Skills, Delivery Skills, Practice

Presentation anxiety usually tops the lists of people's fears. Presentation anxiety is a complicated phenomenon that reflects a triangle of terror. The triangle of terror represents three interacting components of presentation anxiety and how they affect your head, heart, and habits. Understanding your level of presentation anxiety and becoming more confident require an appreciation of all three components.

Head: What kind of fearful thoughts do you have about presentation speaking?
Heart: What kind of emotional and physical distress have you experienced before, during, and even after a presentation?
Habits: To what extent have you mastered the seven principles of presentation speaking?

Your analysis of and answers to these questions can help you to decide on a strategy that will transform the triangle of terror into presentation

Head: Develop a realistic assessment of your attitudes and beliefs about public speaking.
Heart: Analyze where, when, and why you experience emotional and physical distress.
Habits: Keep working to improve your preparation and delivery skills.

Thinking it Over

Analyze what your head, heart, and habits are, and make your own triangle of terror with detailed examples. Make a group of two and help your partner to complete the triangle of strategy.

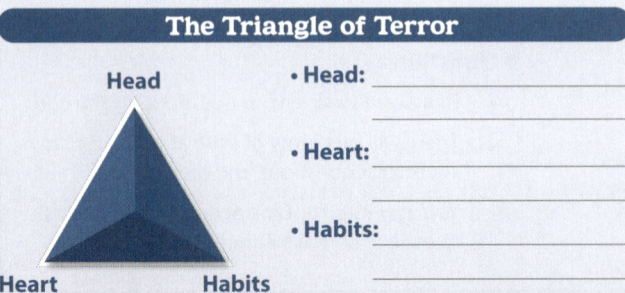

The Triangle of Terror
- Head: _____
- Heart: _____
- Habits: _____

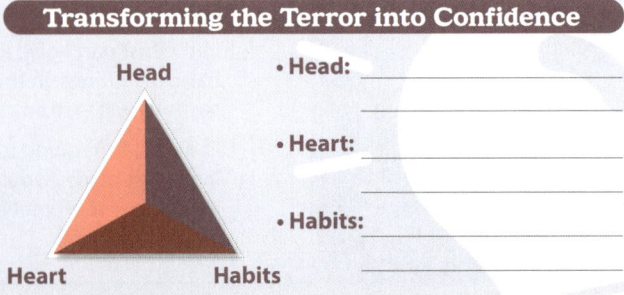

Transforming the Terror into Confidence
- Head: _____
- Heart: _____
- Habits: _____

Linking the Parts

In Unit 4, you learn how to…
- effectively organize a presentation
- arrange your ideas and information for presentation
- determine how to present the material to your audience

Getting Started

John is having the best day of his life. What do you think happened to him? Make a story and present for at least 1 minute.

Warm-up Questions

1. Why is organization so important in one's presentation?

2. Do you use any strategies when organizing your presentation?

Unit 04

Linking the Parts

1. FYI: Background Knowledge

Organizing is Everything

Organization Basics

Once you have gathered all the information you desire to present to the audience, you need to determine how to present the material effectively. There are three methods of approach: deductive, inductive, or a combination of the two.

Deductive approach

This type of presentation is structured in a lecture format and it is the easiest to present. The point of this method is to gather ideas and **pass it onto the audience.** Subsequently, you tell the audience what to do or how to use the information you just presented. This method **leaves little room for** questions and answers.

Inductive approach

This type of presentation allows a little room for flexibility. This approach is good to use when you want to get the **audience to participate.** In this format, you help the audience reach a **conclusion** or a consensus based on the dialogue with your audience. You present examples, events or issues and then ask the group to help you determine the principle.

Combination approach

This type of approach takes longer and involves greater audience participation. You discuss an idea, **reach a conclusion** and then advise your audience what to do **based on the group** consensus. In this method, you suggest instances, events or issues and ask your audience to help you determine the principle. Based on the information you gather, you tell your audience how to proceed.

Practice. Let's recap background knowledge

1 Effective Organization: Rearrange the words to create a sentence.

a) onto / and pass them / the audience / is to gather / ideas / The point / approach / of deductive

b) to use when / approach / the audiences / is good / get / you want to / to participate. / Inductive

c) approach / instances, / and ask / determine / events / or issues / the principle. / to help you / you suggest / In a combination / your audience

2 Choose which type of organization approach is required for the following. Deductive (D), Inductive (I) or Combination (C).

a) You need to get information on the recent sales from your employees so that you can brainstorm with them and tell them what to do next.

b) Your company is having problems. You need to solve it by discussing it with your CEO and others.

c) You are preparing a teaching lesson for a class of university students.

3 Choose true (T) or false (F).

a) The inductive method is the easiest to present out of the three methods.

b) Having a lot of information is important but organization is essential in relaying the information to the audience.

c) The combination approach doesn't really get the audience involved but rather tells them what to do.

2. Language Focus

Useful Words & Expressions

- Below are expressions and phrases that will help you construct effective presentations.
- Review the expressions and try to use them in the presentation practice section.

> Listed below are useful expressions for linking ideas and sentences during your presentation.

Phrase Bank

Ordering
- Firstly… Secondly…
- First of all… / Then… / Next… / After that… / To start with… / Later… / To finish up…

Linking ideas, and sections/ making transitions
- There are three things we have to consider: one, two, and three. A, B, and C.
- Now let us look at the first aspect which is…
- First of all… / In the first place,…
- That's all I would like to say about… (Subject of part A) Now let us examine more closely…

Outlining options
- There seem to be two possibilities of dealing with this…
- A number of options present themselves at this point…
- What exactly are the benefits?
- On the plus side we can add…
- This is not the only weakness of the plan. We cannot ignore the problems that such an action would create…

Finishing on subject
- We've looked at…
- Now we'll move on to…
- Let me turn now to…
- Now I'd like to discuss…
- Now let's look at…
- Let's consider this more in detail.
- What does this mean for…?

Linking Words

- **Let's start with**
  Let's start with our first point.

- **That brings us to**
  That brings us to the second point.

- **First, Second, Lastly**
  Secondly, it is essential to know these differences.

- **Therefore, However, As a result**
  As a result, it is important to address these issues.

- **Similarly**
  Similarly to our neighboring firm, we have to do the same.

- **In particular, Especially**
  In particular, Apple Inc. has been on the rise in the market.

- **For example, For instance**
  For instance, a little decrease might be a good sign when investing.

- **Generally, As a rule**
  Generally, it is good to keep an eye on the market.

- **To conclude**
  To conclude this presentation……

1 Fill in the blanks using the most appropriate linkers.

✓ In particular	✓ Generally
✓ Similarly	✓ However

a) This year we have lost market share. _____, we are still number 1 in the market.

b) Our competitors are becoming stronger. _____ Falcon, has a joint venture with a renowned French firm.

c) Falcon has reduced its costs by relocating. _____, we must also consider cutting the cost of our premises as well.

3. 3 Steps Building Up

Case Study: Convincing the Town of Calhoun

| Step 1 | Prep-Stage

Read the case study context and the situation. Answer the comprehension questions and brainstorm presentation ideas.

The Context			Real Situation
The Company	**The Presenter**	**The Audience**	**The Presentation**
The global wholesale mall named, W. Inc has been increasing their number of operation near the southern border of the United States. They have located a nice plot of land perfect for the mall to be constructed and have to convince the residents of Calhoun about the benefits of having this mall constructed.	Jason Stewart is the Purchasing Manager who has found this plot of land and has been sent from the main branch to convince the people of the town to agree to the construction of this mall.	Calhoun residents are worried that the construction of this mall will only cause them harm by killing small businesses.	Jason has to organize all the benefits of having this mall constructed for the town of Calhoun. Calhoun is a wonderful town to visit with many beautiful features, however, that alone is not enough to bring in tourists. Jason has to use professional fluency get his points across to the audience with a perfectly organized presentation.

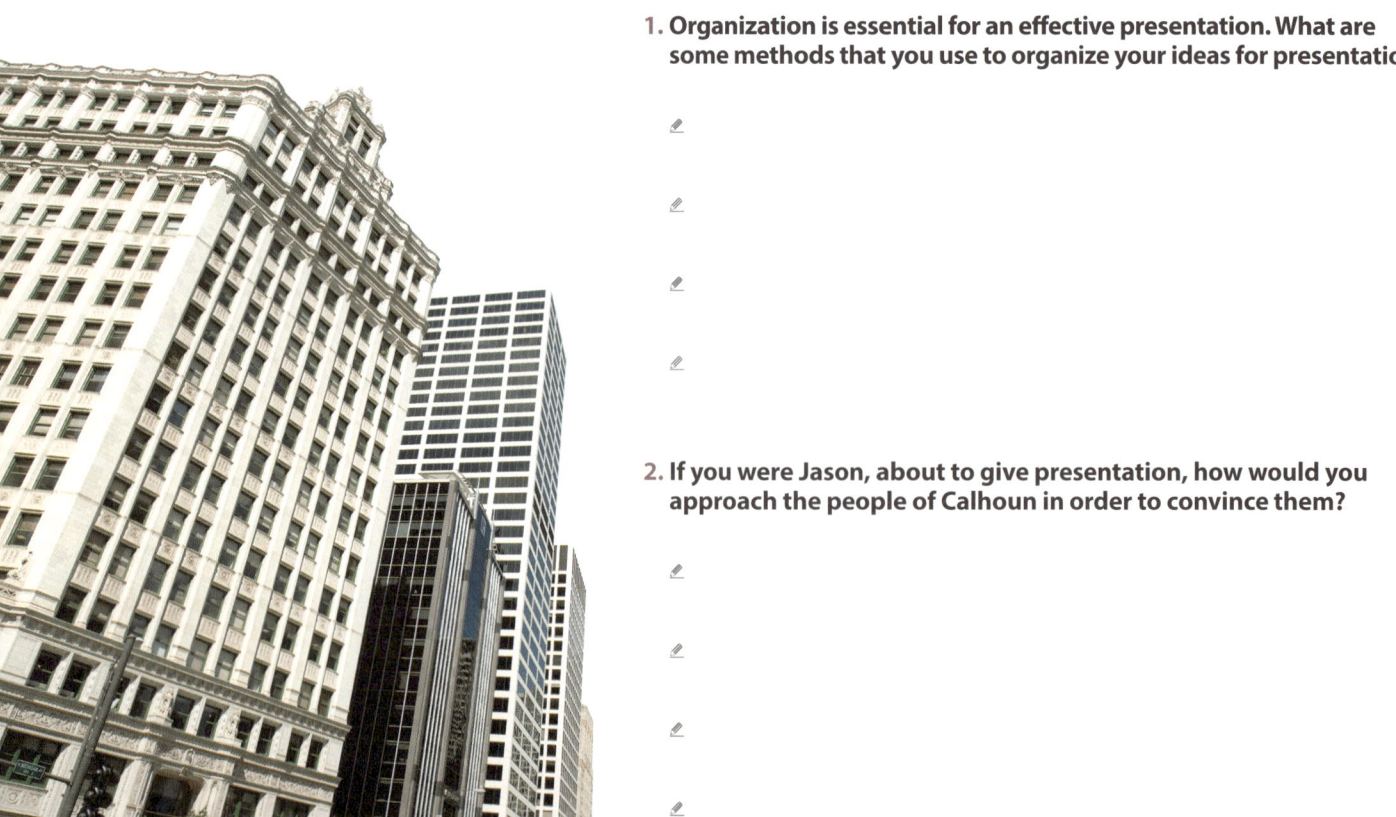

1. Organization is essential for an effective presentation. What are some methods that you use to organize your ideas for presentation?

✎

✎

✎

✎

2. If you were Jason, about to give presentation, how would you approach the people of Calhoun in order to convince them?

✎

✎

✎

✎

Step 2 | Case Comparison

Read the two case presentations and determine which one is more effective.

Poorly Organized Presentation

Good morning everyone. You are all gathered here today so that I can explain to you why the introduction of our mall to your town will benefit you in every way. There are many advantages like increased job opportunities, tourist attraction and an increase in the annual financial benefit of your town. Clearly it benefits everyone in this town. So let's stop being pessimistic about what harm it will do to your business and take an adventurous leap forward towards the greater good of this town. Thank you.

Well Organized Presentation

Good morning people of Calhoun. My name is Jason and I am the Purchasing Manager of W. Inc. I have asked you all to gather here today to announce the construction of our W. Inc. Mall. Many of you are probably skeptical over what kind of benefits we can bring to your town. The following points illustrate on how the mall will benefit the town. Firstly, Calhoun has been known for their beautiful environment, however, is not known to tourists. Our mall will give the town the extra attention that is needed to influence tourists to come visit. Secondly, the construction of our mall will provide many job opportunities. Lastly, the introduction of our mall will help the town with significant financial improvement. Therefore, we believe that we will only do your town good rather than harm. Thank you.

1. **Based on the rubric criteria, score the two cases and add up the total score.**

Type	Unsatisfactory	Poor	Fair/Average	Good	Excellent
Score	1	2	3	4	5
Explain the objectives					
Used transitional phrases					
Presented the problem					
Signalled the beginning of each parts					
Talked about the topic					
Signalled end of each parts					
Highlighted the main ideas					

» Case 1 Total Score :

» Case 2 Total Score :

2. **Listen to the presentation. As you listen, pay attention to and make notes if necessary on how smooth the transition is. Notice how he states all the points in an organized manner which makes it sound very convincing.**

| **Step 3** | **Follow Up**

Use the speech from Jason to write down how he divided up his presentation according to the general structure of a presentation.

Organizational Tools

The following tools can help you arrange your ideas and information into a well-organized presentation with a clear beginning, middle, and end.

◆ **Preliminary Outlines**
   Outlines give you a clear and logical framework on which you hang your ideas and supporting material. They begin in a preliminary form with a few basic building blocks. A well-structured preliminary outline puts the major pieces of your message in a clear and logical order.

◆ **Chunking**
   Chunking is a process of sorting the ideas and supporting material you have gathered for a presentation into unique categories or 'chunks'. This process requires time for recording, sorting and critical thinking, however, it is known as the best way to find an effective, organized pattern for the presentation. <u>There are five steps for chunking:</u>

| Record separate items on separate cards | Sort the cards into unique categories | Reconsider the leftovers | Evaluate the categories | Link card groups to key points |

Review

1. **Organization Basics: Fill in the blanks.**

   a The deductive approach is to gather ideas and _____ the audience.

   This approach leaves _____ for questions and answers.

   b The inductive approach is good to use when you want to get the _____.

   This approach helps the audience to reach a _____.

   c The combination approach involves greater participation from the audience. Here you discuss an idea, _____, and then advise the audience the solution _____ consensus.

2. **Put the chunking process in the correct order.**

a	b	c	d	e
Reconsider the leftovers	Link card groups to key points	Record separate items on separate cards	Sort the cards into unique categories	Evaluate the categories

3. **Organization Tools: Answer the following questions**

   a What are the three main methods of organizational approach?

   1.

   2.

   3.

   b What is the purpose of a preliminary outline when organizing?

   1.

   2.

   3.

Presentation On Stage

Step 1 | Presentation Practice

Use the information below to organize and give a short presentation to the class on why you should get a promotion.

◎ Situation

You are having a meeting with your boss and the board of executives and you want to convince them that you are worthy of the managerial position which just opened up couple days ago. There are many candidates, so you need to organize all of your performance and achievements that have helped the company and relay the information to them.

◎ Your accomplishment for the company thus far:

- Increased your customers by 55% which was the highest throughout all employees in the company.
- Recruited multiple VIP investors to join our venture.
- Assisted in the development of the new subdivision in India.
- Created outreach programs with the community to better the company's image.
- Resolved a major issue with an opposing company in terms of copy-right infringement.
- Have been on an overseas business trip for one year to India for the new subdivision.
- Obtained contracts with the local businesses to use the company's products.
- Helped organize a team-building workshop earned a 5-star rating in a local newspaper.

✓ Checklist for Effective Organization

- ☐ Explain the objectives
- ☐ Use transitional phrases
- ☐ Present related information
- ☐ Signal the beginning of each part
- ☐ Talk about the topic
- ☐ Signal the end of each part
- ☐ Highlight the main points
- ☐ Outline the main ideas in point forms
- ☐ Alert the audience the end of the main part.

Step 2 | Evaluate Yourself & Others

Mark △ for yourself and mark ○ to evaluate others.

Evaluating Presentation Performance

Objectives	1	2	3	4	5
· Did you provide the audience with the objective of your topic at hand					
· Was it clearly stated/easy to understand the purpose of this topic					

Background information	1	2	3	4	5
· Did you provide background information					
· Was there enough information before getting to the main idea					

Main points	1	2	3	4	5
· Was your main point strong enough to convince the audience					
· Did you show them any evidences/examples					

Supporting points	1	2	3	4	5
· Was the supporting points convincing					
· Did it clear up any loose ends that were left from the main point					

Outline/summation	1	2	3	4	5
· Did you summarize the overall idea at the end					
· Was the result convincing enough to be the correct solution of the purpose					

Transition	1	2	3	4	5
· Did you use transitional words or phrases to connect your ideas together					
· Was the flow of your presentation smooth					

» Your Score: _____   » Others: _____

Let's Recap!

Check to see if you have used any of the phrases from the Phrase Bank.

* Remember! Using these phrases will help you deliver a more effective presentation.

◆ Ordering
- ☐ Firstly… Secondly…
- ☐ First of all… / Then… / Next… / After that… / To start with… / Later… / To finish up…

◆ Linking ideas, and sections/ making transitions
- ☐ There are three things we have to consider: one, two, and three. A, B, and C.
- ☐ Now let us look at the first aspect which is…
- ☐ First of all… / In the first place,…
- ☐ That's all I would like to say about…. (Subject of part A) Now let us examine more closely…

◆ Outlining options
- ☐ There seem to be two possibilities of dealing with this…
- ☐ A number of options present themselves at this point…
- ☐ What exactly are the benefits?
- ☐ On the plus side we can add…
- ☐ This is not the only weakness of the plan. We cannot ignore the problems that such an action would create…

◆ Finishing on subject
- ☐ We've looked at…
- ☐ Now we'll move on to…
- ☐ Let me turn now to…
- ☐ Now I'd like to discuss…
- ☐ Now let's look at…
- ☐ Let's consider this more in detail.
- ☐ What does this mean for…?

The Golden Rules for Unit 4

The Basics:
Effective Presentation Organization

I. Introduction

A Purpose/Topic

B Central Idea

C Brief Preview of Key Points
1. Key Point #1
2. Key Point #2
3. Key Point #3

II. Body of the Presentation

A Key Point #1
1. Supporting Material
2. Supporting Material

B Key Point #2
1. Supporting Material
2. Supporting Material

C Key Point #3
1. Supporting Material
2. Supporting Material

Thinking it Over

1. Have you used the presentation organization method presented above?

2. Do you have your own ways of organizing information such as presentation, class notes, etc?

A Picture is Worth a thousand Words

In Unit 5, you will learn how to…
- utilize visual materials
- effectively deliver the visual materials
- give a presentation using minimal words

Getting Started

Today is a special day for May and Tom. What do you think is the special occasion? Make a story and present for at least 1 minute.

Warm-up Questions

1. Why do you think presenting visuals is important in a presentation?

2. What do you think is more informative; words or pictures?

Unit 05

A Picture is Worth A 1000 Words

1. FYI: Background Knowledge

Speaking Visually: Are Pictures Necessary for Presentations?

The Role of Visual Aids

The history of human communication has been evolving with the advancement of technology. From oral communication to text-based, our method of communication has been shifted towards image-centralization. The following are some advantages of visual communication over text-based communication.

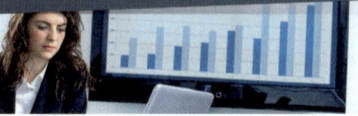

In a study on how we **take in information** during a presentation, Professor Albert Mehrabian, a communication specialist, concluded that 55% of the information that we receive is from visuals while only 7% is text-based.

In a study at the Wharton Research Centre, they were able to identify that pictures were 5 times more **memorable** then bullet points after 3 days. Thus the bullet points were not as effective as pictures are in terms of information residing in one's mind.

In a study by Decker Communication, they reported that the use of visuals in presentation doubles the chance of the presenter **achieving his or her goal** of the presentation, whether it is sales, a job interview, and so on.

Pictures provide a method to relay your message to the audience by **intensifying persuasiveness** of the message. However, this is a very **delicate system** where in order to communicate your message to its **fullest potential**; one must choose a **precise visual aid.** The most **suitably selected** image will greatly increase the **effectiveness** and the **delivery** of your presentation.

Practice. Let's recap background knowledge.

1 Fill in the blanks using the bolded words from the background knowledge article.

- intensifying persuasiveness
- take in information
- visual communication
- suitably selected

a) The pictures can bring forth _____ of the message making the speaker and his information more trustworthy.

b) The most _____ images are the ones that will get the message across to the audience.

c) With our method of relaying message shifting towards _____, effective usage of visual aids is important in one's presentation.

2 Choose true (T) or false (F).

a) Not only are visual aids memorable, but they are also useful in achieving one's goals.

b) Our brain prefers bullet points over images.

c) We take in information much easier when visual aids are supporting the message.

2. Language Focus

Phrase Bank

There are many ways to guide the audience through an image, graph, and slides. The following are some useful phrases you could implement when using visual aids.

Referring to what you will say

- We will see this a little later on.
- This will be the subject of part three.
- We will go into more detail on that later.
- For now it is sufficient to say.

Explaining visual materials

- As you can see here, …
- The chart / slide / table / graph on the following slide shows…
- To illustrate this, let's have a closer look at…
- This graph shows you…
- Please take a look at this…
- This chart illustrates the figures…
- The vertical / horizontal axis represents…

Highlighting the information

- As you can see…
- This clearly shows …
- From this, we can understand how / why…
- This area of the chart is interesting …
- I'd like us to focus our attention on…
- If you look more closely at…

Useful Words & Expressions

- Below are useful information about presentation visuals. Try to incorporate the information in your presentation.

Pointing out Trends

◆ **degree of change**
Considerably/slightly
The trend has considerably risen in the past two years.

◆ **describing direction of change**
Fallen / flattened / remained / rose, To go up / to go down, To decrease / increase, A downturn / a rise, To hit bottom / To reach a peak
The stock market has remained constant for Blackberry.

◆ **speed of change**
Slowly / rapidly
M&B Inc. has been rapidly increasing their product value in the past decade.

◆ **cause and effect**
- What's the reason for this drastic increase?
- The unexpected drop was caused by…
- This was because of…
- As a consequence/result

Terminology for graphs and charts

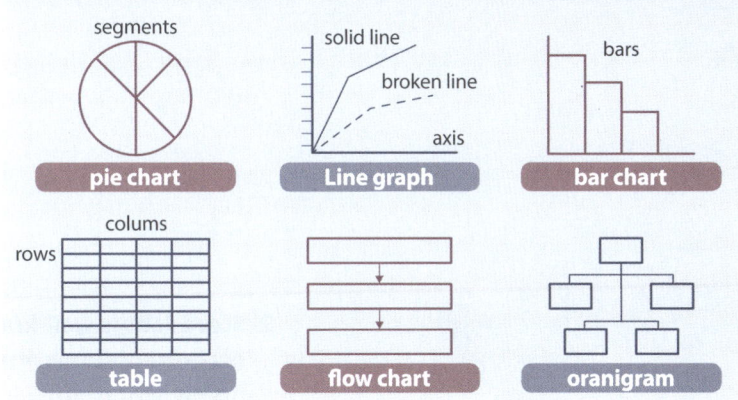

1 Match the descriptive terms to the correct trends.

3. 3 Steps Building Up

Case Study: Presenting a Revolutionary Device

| Step 1 | Prep-Stage

Read the case study context and the situation. Answer the comprehension questions and brainstorm presentation ideas.

The Context			Real Situation
The Company	**The Presenter**	**The Audience**	**The Presentation**
Apple Inc. is an American multinational corporation which develops and markets computer software, consumer electronics, and computers. They have recently developed a new device and are presenting this device at a conference.	Steve Jobs, the CEO of Apple Inc, is a well known American entrepreneur and inventor of almost every Apple product being used today. He has astonished the world with many of his inventions such as the Macintosh and iPod. He has initiated a conference to present his new product, the iPhone.	The audience is composed of the consumers and admirers of Steve Jobs and his company. The audiences have gathered from all over the world. Many media, various CEOs, and investors are present in this conference.	Steve is introducing to the world a new revolutionary communication device, the iPhone. This device, he believes, will change the way people live and will further the advancement of human-technology relationships. His presentation is about 10 minutes.

1. **When you make presentations, what is the percentage of visuals that you use? 10%? 90%? When in the presentation, do you use visuals?**

   ✎

   ✎

   ✎

   ✎

2. **Steve Jobs is well-known for his presentations. Why do you think his presentations attract people? What do you remember about his presentation?**

   ✎

   ✎

   ✎

   ✎

| Step 2 | Case Comparison

Read the two case presentations and determine which one is more effective.

Visual 1

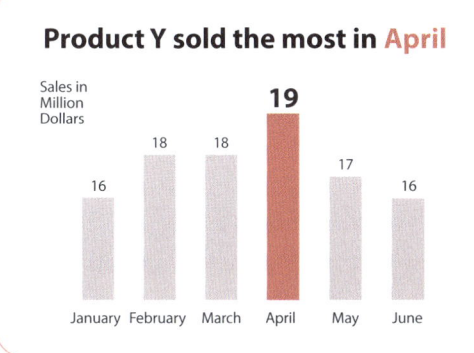

Visual 2

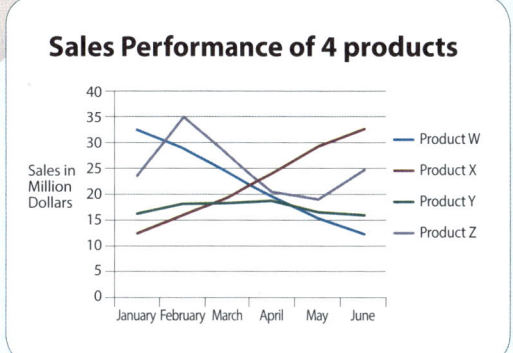

1. **Watch video:** http://www.youtube.com/watch?v=EEEPkThgKM4
   As you watch, pay attention to the visuals and score the rubric.

Type Score	Unsatisfactory 1	Poor 2	Fair/Average 3	Good 4	Excellent 5
Information from visuals were presented effectively	☐	☐	☐	☐	☐
Enhancing the message via visuals	☐	☐	☐	☐	☐
Visuals supported thesis	☐	☐	☐	☐	☐
Legible texts	☐	☐	☐	☐	☐
Effective Headlines	☐	☐	☐	☐	☐
Simple design and content	☐	☐	☐	☐	☐
Reduced text load	☐	☐	☐	☐	☐
Prepared audience for the visuals	☐	☐	☐	☐	☐

2. Steve Jobs is known to be a great story teller. Watch his presentation again and list descriptive words that he uses in his presentation.

| **Step 3** | **Follow Up**

Use the space given below to write down how his slides are different in comparison to poorly chosen visual presentations and your presentation.

Steve Job's Presentation.

1

Poorly chosen visual presentations.

2

My Presentation.

3

Checklist for Effective Visual Aids

1. Ensure all visuals are used effectively to enhance the message, support the thesis, and convey meaning.
2. Make sure text is legible (appropriate style, size, color)
3. Provide effective headlines.
4. Keep design and content simple.
5. Reduce text to a minimum.
6. Prepare the audience for visuals.
7. Present information from the visuals clearly.

Review

1. **Describing Trends: Fill in the blanks with the words provided.**

   - flattened
   - considerably
   - slightly
   - rose

   ⓐ Our sales _____ last year

   ⓑ Sales have _____ out.

   ⓒ Absenteeism has dropped _____ since last month.

   ⓓ Our profits have only _____ increased.

2. **Types of Visuals: Mark the correct names of the graphs presented below.**

   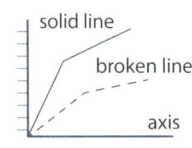
   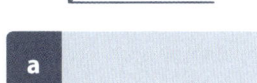

   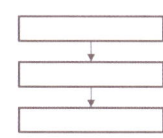

3. **Why Visuals: Rearrange the words to create a sentence.**

   ⓐ superior / are / more / communication / capabilities. / far / in the / Pictures

   ⓑ information / through / digest / pictures. / better / We / can

   ⓒ will greatly / the delivery. / of / the effectiveness / increase / selected / Suitably / images

Presentation On Stage

Step 1 — **Presentation Practice**

You are going to give a presentation about NIKE's rise to fame. Prepare a short presentation and design effective charts or graphs incorporating the information provided below.

◎ **Nike Inc.**

- **Foundation:** 1972
- **Employees:** 45 (1972); 6500 (1992) ; ~40,000 (2012)
- **Sales:** $3.2 million (1972); $3.4 billion (1992); $25 billion (2012)
- **Share price:** $5.50 per share (1980), $65.00 per share (1992) ; $75.91 per share (2012)

◎ **Total world-wide Revenue from 2012**

- **Footwear:** $14.53 billion (58%)
- **Apparel:** $6.82 billion (27%)
- **Others:** $3.65 billion (15%)

Based on the information above, create a 1 page presentation slide.

» **Presentation Slide**

Based on what you wrote in the presentation slide, write a script to go with it.

» **Presentation Script**

✓ Checklist for Effective Organization

- ☐ All visuals are used effectively to enhance message
- ☐ Visuals supported the thesis and conveyed the message
- ☐ Texts were legible
- ☐ Provided effective headlines
- ☐ Kept design and content simple
- ☐ Reduced text to minimum
- ☐ Prepared the audience for the visuals
- ☐ Presented the information from the visuals effectively

Step 2 | Evaluate Yourself & Others

Mark △ for yourself and mark ○ to evaluate others.

Evaluating Presentation Performance

Appropriateness | 1 | 2 | 3 | 4 | 5
- Were the pictures appropriate for the message to be delivered
- Was the picture easy enough for the audience to understand

Informative image | 1 | 2 | 3 | 4 | 5
- Was the visual aid informative
- Did the image relate to the topic at hand
- Did you use minimal words in your presentation

Enough visual aid | 1 | 2 | 3 | 4 | 5
- Did you bombard the audience with too many images
- Did you have enough visual aids to guide the audience through the presentation

Explain the image | 1 | 2 | 3 | 4 | 5
- Did you convey your idea through the image
- Was the message of the image well explained in detail
- Do you think the audience understood the chosen image

Synchronization | 1 | 2 | 3 | 4 | 5
- Was your oral speech on the same page as the visual aid
- Did you make sure to check if your oral part was synchronized with your presentation flow

Transition between images | 1 | 2 | 3 | 4 | 5
- Was the flow of your slides smooth
- Did you present your images as if you're telling them a story

» Your Score: _____   » Others: _____

Let's Recap!

Check to see if you have used any of the phrases from the Phrase Bank.

*Remember! Using these phrases will help you deliver a more effective presentation.

◆ **Referring to what you will say**
- ☐ We will see this a little later on.
- ☐ This will be the subject of part three.
- ☐ We will go into more detail on that later.
- ☐ For now it is sufficient to say.

◆ **Explaining visual materials**
- ☐ As you can see here, …
- ☐ The chart / slide / table / graph on the following slide shows…
- ☐ To illustrate this, let's have a closer look at…
- ☐ This graph shows you…
- ☐ Please take a look at this…
- ☐ This chart illustrates the figures…
- ☐ The vertical / horizontal axis represents…

◆ **Highlighting the information**
- ☐ As you can see…
- ☐ This clearly shows …
- ☐ From this, we can understand how/why…
- ☐ This area of the chart is interesting …
- ☐ I'd like us to focus our attention on…
- ☐ If you look more closely at…

The Golden Rules for Unit 5

Utilizing Images to its Fullest Potential.

① Using visual aids helps the presenter in getting cues to which slide comes next.

② Your message is more important than the picture.

③ Pictures can be used for decorative purposes. However, they can also be distracting.

④ Use the images to tell a story. When done correctly, the audience will be interested throughout the whole presentation.

⑤ Make sure to explain every image. The audience will be lost if you just show a picture and don't explain.

⑥ If possible, keep the texts to a minimum.

⑦ Make sure to keep the images simple. If they are too complex, you will lose the audience.

 Thinking it Over

1. What kinds of presentation aids have you used previously? Why did you use them?

2. What kind of presentation aids and media do you think are the most effective?

Powerful Delivery

In Unit 6, you will learn how to…
- use body language for effective presentations
- have control of yourself to give presentations successfully
- look confident using appropriate presentation skills

Getting Started

Two business partners are shaking hands to seal a deal after they've been discussing the matter several times this year. What do you think the deal was about? Make a story and present for at least 1 minute.

Warm-up Questions

1. What are some tools you use to look confident during a presentation?

2. What is the main tool for an excellent presentation?

Unit 06

Powerful Delivery

1. FYI: Background Knowledge

Stage Presence: What Is It and How Can I Get It?

Stage presence is presenting in a relaxed manner from your heart. You can be dramatic, comedic, anything you desire. You have stage presence when you transform yourself and the audience says, "Wow, that's amazing!"

Four areas to focus on to develop stage presence

Business people often talk about the value of bringing a **commanding presence** into the room or onto the stage. Some people have been given special **genetic advantages** in this area, having been blessed with a dashing physique, or a voice as rich and deep as some voice actors. That doesn't mean the rest of us are out of luck. There are things we have control over that can make us more commanding figures in the boardroom and on the dais. They include:

Energy control	Voice/Volume control:	Eye Contact:	Posture & gestures:
Presenting in front of a live audience and feedback community is excellent practice for stage presence. Practice **impromptu storytelling** and **externalizing your voice** as often as possible with a few audio and video tools (smart phone apps included). Keep your recordings private if that's preferred.	Be sure to speak **at a volume that fills the room.** That increases the energy level and keeps your audience more alert. If you have a soft voice, use a microphone and make sure your sound engineer knows you want the speaker system kept on the loud side.	Make eye contact, and make it **direct and persistent** enough that it says to audience members, "I see you and I'm paying attention to you."	**Enlarge and animate** our physical self with arm gestures above the waist and extending away from the body.

Practice. Let's recap background knowledge

1 Make sentences using the chunks from the article above.

   a) genetic advantages: _____

   b) impromptu storytelling: _____

   c) commanding presence: _____

2 Match the words with correct meanings.

   persistent •   • a) impart motion or activity to inspire to action
   animate •   • b) project or attribute to external circumstances or causes
   enlarge •   • c) continuing firmly or obstinately in a course of action in spite of difficulty or opposition
   externalize • • d) make or grow larger in size, scope; expand

3 Create a 30-second speech using the following words.

   a) direct and persistent / commanding presence / externalize   b) genetic advantages / enlarge / impromptu

2. Language Focus

Vocab Bank

Action words
Powerful verbs that describe the effort you used to complete a task

Acronym
an abbreviation formed from the initial components in a phrase or a word

Infobesity
information overload

Perception
the ability to see, hear, or become aware of something through the senses

1. Give some examples of action words.

2. Create a short speech using some action words you chose.

3. Give the speech you prepared after adding words that are more emotional (ask classmates first for suggestions).

Use "Real" Words in your Business Presentation

Try to choose and use words that are **Correct, Simple, Emotional,** and **Visual.**

1. If you are talking about a mushroom, call it a mushroom. Not a squirrel. If you're talking about video, call it video, not media. If you're talking about a problem, call it a problem, not a challenge. **Choose correct words to deliver your meaning.**

2. Using simple words has a simple standard. Would your average 8-yr old understand it? Reduce the words to a minimum to get understanding. **Use simple words to make your presentation easier to understand.**

3. Use a word that gets a reaction, like fierce, rather than one that washes over you. **Emotional words create a different perception.**

4. A video is worth one thousand times than a sound-bite because it's a picture painted with words. **Visuals create an experience or a picture in the mind's eye.**

3. 3 Steps Building Up

Case Study: Budget cuts, but how?

| Step 1 | Prep-Stage

Read the case study context and the situation. Answer the comprehension questions and brainstorm presentation ideas.

The Context			Real Situation
The Company	**The Presenter**	**The Audience**	**The Presentation**
The BBDO Group is a multinational media company headquartered in the UK. Mr. Muttha, the new CEO of its New York office, is concerned about the impact of the economic downturn. He decided to call a meeting to prepare their budgets along with department budget cuts for the coming year.	Jack Johnson is the director of the account and production divisions. The purpose of his presentation this time is to convince the audience that budget cuts are expected as an economy downturn is expected; however, what's more important is to cut costs painlessly in business.	Jack is giving the presentation to the senior managers including the new CEO.	Jack has enough experience giving impressive presentations to high level managers, but he needs to really make a pitch for painless and effective budget cuts. The whole team is counting on him, and he doesn't want to let them down.

1. **Do you know anyone with a strong stage presence? What qualities does this person have? What makes them stand out?**

   ✎

   ✎

   ✎

   ✎

2. **Read the context of the presentation.**
   - Imagine you are making the presentations.
     a) Which content will you include?
     b) How will you structure the content?
     c) Rehearse with your team members and get additional ideas for a better stage presence.

   ✎

   ✎

   ✎

   ✎

Step 2 | Case Comparison

Read and listen to the two case presentations and determine which one has a more powerful delivery.

🎧 Case 1

Mr. Muttha's forecast and plan for the next fiscal year will eliminate 40 % of the current jobs in an attempt to alleviate the $3 million budget deficit. These types of decisions are extremely difficult, because behind all the budgetary numbers are the names of dedicated and loyal team members. We're a very close team here at BBDO NY. The cuts will leave us with about 70 employees, which is less than half of the 160 who worked here in the previous year.

VS

🎧 Case 2

First of all, I'd like to thank you all for having me here today. As Mr. Muttha strongly suggested, each and every team needs to focus on reducing labor costs. Let's say your boss calls you in to his or her office and asks you whether you'd consider taking a salary cut in order to keep your job. Surprised? You shouldn't be. As the worldwide recession continues, more and more companies are adopting this strategy in an effort to reduce labor costs while avoiding major layoffs. Whether you, as an employee, should accept the offer depends on your specific needs, in terms of both your career and your personal finances.

1. Below is a checklist for effective body language. You can use the checklist for your presentation.

Body Language	Yes	No
Relax and manage your stress level	☐	☐
Maintain a confident stance and posture	☐	☐
Concentrate on emotions and feelings to deliver your message	☐	☐
Make a confident entrance	☐	☐
Maintain eye contact	☐	☐
Use your hands to express more	☐	☐
Use movement effectively	☐	☐

2. Which presentation case do you think is better? Support your opinion and discuss it with your partner.

| Step 3 | Follow Up

Look at the four elements and write down the key points for each category.

Energy Control

Voice Control

Eye Contact

Posture & Gestures

Pictures of different kinds of effective and ineffective body language:

Do Actions Speak Louder Than Words?

Review each and every picture describing body language and see which one you are familiar with. Good versus Bad!

① Closed vs. Open

closed(x)   open(o)

② Hands Availability: What to do with your hands

③ Eye Contact

④ Gestures with Facial Expressions

Review

1. Match the correct description with the four tips for "real" words

✓ Correct   ✓ Simple   ✓ Emotional   ✓ Visual

a) _____ : Reduce the words to a minimum to get understanding.
b) _____ : It's like a picture painted with words.
c) _____ : Use the right words for what you are presenting.
d) _____ : Use a word that produces effective reaction.

2. Connect the body language tips to the correct example.

1. Make a confident entrance
2. Maintain eye contact
3. Talk with your hands
4. Move to keep an audience from becoming bored

a) Walk toward the audience before making an important point
b) Use more animated gestures
c) Look at specific individuals or small groups and hold their attention briefly. Then move to another group or individual in another part of the room
d) Walk out on stage with good posture, head held high, and a steady, smooth gait.

3. For additional listening practice, you may listen to good case mp3 or read the script below and complete the sentences.

First of all, I'd like to thank you all for having me here today. As Mr. Muttha strongly suggested, each and every team does need to **ⓐ** _____ . Let's say.. Your boss calls you in to his or her office and asks you whether you'd consider **ⓑ** _____ in order to keep your job. Surprised? You shouldn't be. **ⓒ** _____ , more and more companies are adopting this strategy in an effort to reduce labor costs **ⓓ** _____ . Whether you, as an employee, should accept the offer **ⓔ** _____ , both in terms of your career and personal finances.

Answer Key: ⓐ focus on reducing labor costs ⓑ taking a salary cut ⓒ As the worldwide recession continues ⓓ while avoiding major layoffs ⓔ depends on your specific needs

Presentation
On Stage

Step 1

Presentation Practice

You are the Vice President of the company and are giving a speech at the end-of-year Christmas party. Your company went through some tough times and some employees were laid off throughout the year as the whole economy suffered. You have an urge to lift up company morale and prepare for another year with a positive attitude. Prepare a motivational speech for the event.

◎ **Who is the audience, and what is the purpose of the event?**

Employees are looking forward to the traditional work Christmas party, which is a wonderful way for a business to celebrate its ups and downs for the year. To make employees feel appreciated, you have a responsibility to give a perfect speech to encourage them so that employees get an opportunity to share the joys of the season.

» **Key Message for your Speech**

✓ Checklist for Effective Body Language

- ☐ Relax and manage your stress level.
- ☐ Maintain confident stance and posture.
- ☐ Concentrate on emotions and feelings to deliver your message.
- ☐ Make a confident entrance.
- ☐ Maintain eye contact.
- ☐ Talk with your hands.
- ☐ Use movement effectively.

Step 2 | Evaluate Yourself & Others

Mark △ for yourself and mark ○ to evaluate others.

Evaluating Presentation Performance

Confidence Level	1	2	3	4	5
· Manage stress level well					
· Speak clearly with correct articulation and the right vocal tone control					
· Make a confident entrance					
· Maintain a confident stance and posture					

Focused Delivery	1	2	3	4	5
· Voice					
· Posture					
· Gestures					
· Eye contact					

Language	1	2	3	4	5
· Accurate					
· Appropriate					
· Simple/ easy to understand					

Overall	1	2	3	4	5
· Appropriate for subject and audience					
· Proper examples					
· Appropriate visual aids					
· Well managed emotions and feelings					

» **Your Score:** _____   » **Others:** _____

Let's Recap!

Check to see if you have used any of the phrases from the Phrase Bank.

*Remember! Using these phrases will help you deliver a more effective presentation.

◆ **Action words**
☐ Powerful verbs that describe the effort you used to complete a task

1. Give some examples of action words.

◆ **Acronym**
☐ an abbreviation formed from the initial components in a phrase or a word

2. Create a short speech using some action words you chose.

◆ **Infobesity**
☐ information overload

3. Give the speech you prepared after adding words that are more emotional (ask classmates first for suggestions).

◆ **Perception**
☐ the ability to see, hear, or become aware of something through the senses

The Golden Rules for Unit 6

Tips for Effective Body Language on Stage

1. Manage your stress level
2. Get involved emotionally
3. Make a confident entrance
4. Maintain eye contact
5. Get out from behind the lectern
6. Talk with your hands
7. Move to keep an audience from becoming bored

Thinking it Over

1. Which of these tips do you find most useful? What tips can people use to turn stage fright into stage presence?

2. Have you ever faced any cultural issues while giving a presentation? How did you react to successfully end the presentation?

Adding a Special Touch

In Unit 7, you will learn how to…
- deliver audience-friendly presentations
- spice up speeches or presentations using a good sense of humor

Getting Started

Team members are applauding a good presentation at the end of a meeting. Talk about the best presentation you've recently seen or heard. Present for at least 1 minute.

Warm-up Questions

1. How do you handle interruptions and distractions during a presentation?

2. How do people make audiences laugh during presentations?

Unit 07

Adding a Special Touch

1. FYI: Background Knowledge

Dealing with a Distracted Audience

It's not easy speaking to an audience of people who appear to be **distracted** by their cell phones, or are **clattering away** on their laptops. We have all been to conferences where people seemed to pay more attention to their electronic devices than to the live person on the podium. As smartphones connect people to their busy lives, this **phenomenon** will only become more common.

This distraction **epidemic** calls for a different type of approach — one that can **engage people,** not just force them to stare silently. Here is what you can do to capture the attention of a distracted audience.

Let Down Your Guard

Some people learn best by doing something else while listening, whether it's doodling or using a phone. When you **spot** someone on his or her phone while you are speaking, take a positive view that this is a person who's taking notes, or tweeting what a great speaker you are, or perhaps the individual is someone who needs to do something with his or her hands to pay attention.

Encourage Participation

When the audience is involved, they are more engaged. **Make use of** their distraction and include it in the presentation. A relaxed speaking environment is enjoyable for the audience. Make a connection and give the audience a better environment for learning.

Practice. Let's recap background knowledge

1 Use the chunks from the article to make up sentences.

a) put off:

b) clatter away:

c) make use of:

2 Match the words with correct meanings.

phenomenon • • a) unable to concentrate and having one's attention diverted

epidemic • • b) something that can be observed and studied and that typically is unusual or difficult to explain fully

distracted • • c) see, notice, or recognize someone or something that is difficult to detect or that one is searching for

spot • • d) a fact or situation that is observed to exist or happen, especially one whose cause or explanation is in question.

3 Work in groups. Share and connect through stories about your experiences facing distractions in presentations. Make a list of things you can do to engage your audience during a presentation.

Ex) Let your audience support the point you're making with their first-hand experiences

a)

b)

c)

2. Language Focus

Phrase Bank

Listed below are useful expressions for guiding the audience throughout the presentation. Try to use them during your presentation practices.

Referring to what you have said previously

- As I have already said earlier…
- As we saw in part one…
- To repeat what I've said so far…

Asking rhetorical questions

- Have you ever seen / heard / experienced…?
- How can we explain this? What does that mean?
- What can be done about that?
- What does this imply for you, as a consumer?

Coping with problems

- Sorry, what I meant was …
- Let's recap on that…
- Sorry, perhaps I didn't make that clear.
- So, just to give you the main points here…

Useful Words & Expressions

- Below are expressions and words that will help you construct effective presentations.
- Review the expressions and try to use them in the presentation practice section.

Using Colorful Language

◆ **Use Vivid Verbs:**

e.g. He planned to change the procedure.
→ He planned to alter the procedure.

The harder you worked, the more you disliked your job.
→ The harder you toiled, the more you detested your job.

Good	Bad
· craft / build / create	· make
· alter / upgrade / transform / adapt	· change
· employ / labor / toil / slave	· work

◆ **Avoid Weak / Vague Verbs and Use Stronger Linking Verbs:**

e.g. The sunset was magnificent. → The sunset looked magnificent.
I went to the store. → I drove to the store.

Good	Bad
· Seem / appear / feel / grow / look / sound	· Be / have / do / go · There is / there are

◆ **Use words that can make your story memorable:**

e.g. The house was on fire. → Flames erupted from the windows.

The breeze blew the leaves on the trees.
→ The breeze lifted the leaves on the trees.

My coworker saw the traffic accident that occurred on I-85.
→ My co-worker witnessed the traffic accident that occurred on I-85.

1 Revise the words in red and rewrite the examples using colorful language.

a **There is** no harm in using cellular phones inside the hospital.
(Avoid "there is / are")

b This has **the tendency** to make log browsing a tedious and ineffective process. (Avoid using weak verbs.)

c My boss **walked slowly** towards the door after the conversation. (Use words that can make your story memorable.)

3. 3 Steps Building Up

Case Study: New Product Launch

| Step 1 | Prep-Stage

Read the case study context and the situation. Answer the comprehension questions and brainstorm presentation ideas.

The Company

QNP Ltd is one of the leading electronics manufacturers, and recently it came out with a super-light, ultra-thin laptop. The problem is that there are many top brands that have recently launched their best ultra thin laptops as well. QNP Ltd needs to prove that their product remains competitive.

The Presenter

Kurt McGill is the CEO of QNP Ltd. He announced this morning that he is going to introduce the new revolutionary product to the world on the launching date.

The Audience

Early adopters are the target audience because they are always on the early edge of trends, but basically anybody who is interested in QNP's new product is invited to the presentation. Some audience members waited in line hours before the presentation began.

1. **Check out the tips for capturing audience's attention (from Unit 2) and chooses tips that you want to use in you presentation. Explain your reasoning.**

   ✎

   ✎

   ✎

   ✎

2. **Imagine you are Kurt McGill, about to give a presentation on the company's new product. What are some key points that you want to include in your presentation? How would you appeal to your audience?**

   ✎

   ✎

   ✎

   ✎

Step 2 | Case Comparison

Read the two case presentations and determine which one is more effective.

🎧 Case 1

This winter, we decided to deliver this 13.3-inch laptop that's lighter, thinner and packs a more up-to-date processor than a MacBook Air. Also, we paid more attention to better quality at a lower price. With your choice of color, you may enjoy hands-on control with a Full HD1 touch screen and built-in speakers. With all that miniaturization and speed, of course, there's a price premium too.

🎧 Case 2

What is it like to hold it in your hands? Look how I am holding it. It's awesome, isn't it! Beyond its beauty, as a practical matter, this laptop boots in 12 seconds. Thinner than an inch, lighter than "AIR"! And on top of it all, absolutely charismatic along with the choice of elegant colors that adds to the charm. The beauty of it all, thought, is the price. Get a close-up look at this skinny lappie!

1. Based on the rubric criteria, check to see which presentation is better. (Case 1 or Case 2)

Type	Bad Presentation Skills	Good Presentation Skills
Visual Aids	☐	☐
Tone of Voice	☐	☐
Easy to Understand	☐	☐
Enthusiasm / Passion	☐	☐
Storytelling	☐	☐
Humor	☐	☐
Other Engaging Skills	☐	☐
Overall Quality	☐	☐

2. Which case do you think is better? Support your opinion and discuss it with your partner.

| Step 3 | Follow Up

Work in groups to choose any presentation topic. Then choose the target audience. Finally write down ways to add a special touch to your presentation to engage the audience.

Topic

Target Audience

Ways to Participate

Did You Know?

The Final Touch: **Add Humor to Presentations**

Humor completes your presentation once you build personal rapport with an audience.

e.g. 1
In order to give my words more weight I am taking all of you out to McDonald's after this speech. – *adding jokes*

e.g. 2
Teamwork is the ability to work as a group toward a common vision, even if that vision becomes extremely blurry. – *adding quotation*

Review

1. **Match the correct description with the tools for engaging your audience**

   ✓ Statistics   ✓ Activities   ✓ Metaphors   ✓ Repetitions

   a Repeating key points throughout a presentation

   b Helping the audience get to know one another or gather information

   c Creating a shortcut to understanding and simplifying what is complex

   d Explaining something unfamiliar in terms of figures/numbers the audience already knows about

2. **Phrase Bank: Complete the below sentences using the following phrases.**

   a) As I have already said earlier,…

   »

   b) Have you ever experienced…?

   »

   c) Sorry, what I meant was,…

   »

3. **For additional listening practice, you may listen to good case mp3 or read the script below and complete the sentences.**

   What is it like to **a** ....? Look how I am holding it. It's awesome, isn't it!

   Beyond its beauty, as a practical matter, this laptop **b** .... Thinner than an inch, light than "AIR"! And on top of it all, **c** .... along with the choice of elegant colors that adds to the charm. The beauty of it, though, is the price.

   d .... this skinny lappie!

   Answer Key: ⓐ hold it in your hands ⓑ boots in 12 seconds ⓒ absolutely charismatic ⓓ get a close-up look at

Presentation On Stage

Step 1 — **Plan a presentation**

You are the HR manager of this company, and you have an informative meeting scheduled at 3 p.m. You are giving a speech on the newly established corporate policies, during what is planned to be a one-hour meeting.

◎ Audiences

Employees at ABC LLC (Women's Clothing and Accessories) are not too excited about the meeting scheduled this afternoon because the purpose of the meeting is to announce tighter rules and policies, and every time new policies are in effect, the rules are enforced strictly.

◎ Situation Summary

Because it is Friday afternoon, you'd like to do this with humor. You believe you can make any presentation fun even if it's not the most exciting topic. Your goal is to motivate everyone, not just a handful of employees as you help them understand the purpose of the new policies.

» **In the box below, list some ways and methods you can use to engage the employees.**
- **Presentation Topic:** To give information about newly established corporate policies.
- **Goal:** Engage the audience.
- How will you engage the audience?

✓ Storytelling Checklist

☐ **Purpose and Topic**
: Did the story have a clear and appropriate purpose?

☐ **Audience Analysis**
: Was the story appropriate for the audience? Did the story adapt to audience characteristics, interests, attitudes, etc.? State the topic and title

☐ **Credibility**
: Was the storyteller believable? Did the storyteller convey immediacy and enthusiasm?

☐ **Logistics**
: Was the story appropriate for the occasion and place?

☐ **Content**
: Did the story set the mood, place, and time? Were the characters and plot well developed? Did the storyteller create vivid images? Was the punch line clear?

☐ **Organization**
: Did the story develop logically? Did the introduction establish a mood, motivate interest, and "set the stage"? Did the story end gracefully?

☐ **Performance**
: Did the storyteller use appropriate form(s) of delivery; effective vocal and physical delivery, including eye contact?

Step 2 | Evaluate Yourself & Others

Mark △ for yourself and mark ○ to evaluate others.

Evaluating Presentation Performance

Purpose and Topic	1	2	3	4	5
· Clearly stated					
· Repeatedly stated					
· Humor / stories well-linked to the points					

Audience Analysis	1	2	3	4	5
· Target audience					
· Specific information properly prepared					

Credibility	1	2	3	4	5
· Reliable stories					
· Confident statements					
· Inspiring moments					

Performance	1	2	3	4	5
· Appropriate gestures					
· Appropriate tone of voice					
· Eye contact					

Content	1	2	3	4	5
· Well developed					
· Vivid images to support the topic / purpose					

Organization	1	2	3	4	5
· Logically developed					
· Clearly planned beginning / ending					

» Your Score: _____

» Others: _____

Let's Recap!

Check to see if you have used any of the phrases from the Phrase Bank.

*Remember! Using these phrases will help you deliver a more effective presentation.

◆ **Referring to what you have said previously**
- ☐ As I have already said earlier…
- ☐ As we saw in part one…
- ☐ To repeat what I've said so far…

◆ **Asking rhetorical questions**
- ☐ Have you ever seen / heard / experienced…?
- ☐ How can we explain this? What does that mean?
- ☐ What can be done about that?
- ☐ What does this imply for you, as a consumer?

◆ **Coping with problems**
- ☐ Sorry, what I meant was …
- ☐ Let's recap on that…
- ☐ Sorry, perhaps I didn't make that clear.
- ☐ So, just to give you the main points here…

The Golden Rules for Unit 7

Tips for Engaging

1 Posture and Movement
When the audience finds their energy level dropping, get them to stand up for a few minutes.

2 Repetitions
Skillful presenters use the technique of repeating key points throughout their presentation.

3 Humor
Humor can be effective when used naturally and appropriately.

4 Inside Scoop
Give the audience the most recent, relevant information available on the subject.

5 Personal Experience
Support the point you're making with first-hand experience.

6 Analogies and Metaphors
The more complex your subject, the more important it is to use analogies and metaphors.

7 Storytelling
Everyone has his or her own story and can picture participating in the story while listening.

8 Startling Statistics
Be sure to present only the numbers and statistics that are necessary to make your point.

9 Handouts & Note-taking
Encourage audience members to be creative in their note-taking - rather than simply writing sentences.

10 Games and Activities
Participatory activities help the audience get to know one another or gather information.

Thinking it Over

1. Have you ever fallen asleep during a presentation? Have you ever had someone fall asleep during your presentation?

2. Do you know how to use humor effectively as a presentation skill? How does humor stimulate ideas about the subject during your presentation?

Finishing Strongly

In Unit 8, you will learn how to...
- summarize the main concepts effectively at the end of a presentation
- call attention to the closing of a presentation
- help the audience remember the last few seconds of a presentation

Getting Started

There are no words to describe the feelings of victory when people complete a long race. Talk about a moment when you felt great accomplishment. Present for at least 1 minute.

Warm-up Questions

1. When you give a presentation, how does the audience know you're done?

2. What is the best/worst way to end a presentation?

Unit 08

Finishing Strongly

1. FYI: Background Information

What are the key elements for a strong conclusion?

A strong opener **grabs** your audience's **attention** and leads them to your key messages; a strong close **takes them back** to your key messages and brings your presentation full circle to your ultimate objective.

Can your entire presentation hinge on the final impression you make?

Plan your conclusion.

Your conclusion is a **critical** part of your presentation. It should **reinforce your key messages** and add to **the positive impression** that hopefully you will have created with your audience.

Conclusions should be short.

Don't **ramble.** An ending that drags on can actually undo much of the positive impact of an otherwise good presentation. Once you announce you're about to wind up, don't go on talking and talking.

Make the ending crystal clear.

Your **call to action** should be clear and specific. Your audience should be left with no doubt about what it is you're asking at the conclusion of your presentation.

Make your last impression a lasting one.

People tend to **recall best** what they hear last. So prepare and rehearse your conclusion with special care. Consider how you can make your conclusion **memorable** both in substance and delivery.

Practice. Let's recap background knowledge

1 Use the chunks from the article to make up sentences.

a) call to action: _____

b) grab someone's attention: _____

c) tuck into: _____

2 Match the words with their correct meanings.

- critical • • a) of decisive importance; crucial
- ramble • • b) worth being remembered or noted; remarkable
- obscure • • c) to talk or write in a discursive, aimless manner
- memorable • • d) faintly perceptible as to lack clear delineation; indistinct

3 Create a 1-minute speech using the following words for the given topic.

a) ramble / call to action / memorable (Topic: Improving communication skills at work)

Score: ___/10	Used all 3 words (5 pts)	Consistency (3 pts)	Length of the speech (2 pts)

b) grab attention / obscure / critical (Topic: Lunch time activities)

Score: ___/10	Used all 3 words (5 pts)	Consistency (3 pts)	Length of the speech (2 pts)

2. Language Focus

Listed below are useful expressions for good ways of ending a speech. Try to use them during your presentation practices.

Phrase Bank

Signposting the end of your presentation.

- At this stage I would like to run through / over the main points…
- This brings me to the end of my presentation.
- So, as we have seen today…
- As a result we suggest that…
- In the light of what we have seen today I suggest that…
- In conclusion I would like to say that…
- I would like to finish by reminding everyone that…

Summarizing and concluding

- In conclusion…
- To summarize… / To sum up…
- Let's sum up, shall we?
- Let's summarize briefly what we've looked at…
- Finally, let me remind you of some of the issues we've covered…
- If I can just sum up the main points…
- Before I stop, let me go over the key issues again.
- What I've tried to show in this part…
- To recap what we've seen so far…

Useful Words & Expressions

The following is a list of a the words and phrases that will help you summarize your presentations:

- **An overview of…**
  That's an overview of the main points. Now, just to summarize, let's briefly look at the main points again.

- **Direct attention again to…**
  That concludes my presentation. Let me direct your attention again to the main points.

- **Go over**
  I'd like to quickly go over the main points of today's topic.

- **In any event**
  In any event, your presentation will ideally form a bridge.

- **In a nutshell**
  Well, that brings us to the end of the final section. In a nutshell, new policies will help us improve work efficiency.

- **On the whole**
  On the whole, it would be your responsibility to follow through on the matter.

- **Recap/repeat**
  Before we end, let me briefly recap what we have discussed here today.

- **The bottom line**
  We've discussed many points today, but in short, the bottom line is that we have to get the right things done because nobody else can do it for us.

- **Wrap up / sum up**
  Let me wrap up the main points again before I conclude my presentation.

1 Create a short ending again using one of the above words.

2 Give the speech you prepared and ask classmates for suggestions.

Was it a powerful ending?	1	2	3	4	5
Was it tied to the topic?	1	2	3	4	5
Overall quality of the speech	1	2	3	4	5

3. 3 Steps Building Up

Case Study: End Your Presentation With a BANG!

| Step 1 | Prep-Stage

Read the case study context and the situation. Answer the comprehension questions and brainstorm presentation ideas.

The Context			Real Situation
The Company	**The Presenter**	**The Audience**	**The Presentation**
Gazprom Inc. is Russia's largest company, and the world's biggest natural gas producer. The company just hired entry-level employees through the campus recruiting system.	Alex Miller is the CEO of Gazprom, Russia's largest company, and the world's biggest natural gas producer. He is recognized as one of the 100 best-performing CEOs in the world. Alex is giving a motivational presentation to inspire new employees on their first day.	Students who have just got hired and their parents or family members are invited to the presentation. The audience members are excited about the opportunity because Alex is also known as one of the world's most captivating communicators.	Alex is preparing a presentation that will inspire and encourage the new hires. He'd like to focus on the closing, so he can leave a lasting impression in their minds.

1. **Discuss with your partner some presentations that you've seen with strong/weak conclusions. What did the presenter do?**

   ✎

   ✎

   ✎

   ✎

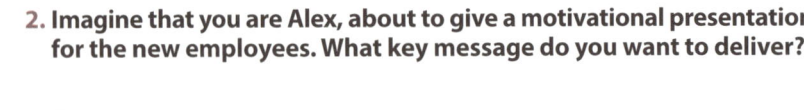

2. **Imagine that you are Alex, about to give a motivational presentation for the new employees. What key message do you want to deliver?**

   ✎

   ✎

   ✎

   ✎

| Step 2 | Case Comparison

Read the two case presentations and determine which one is more effective.

🎧 Case 1

We've discussed many points today. Please check out the summary I have on this last page. Let me read this last page aloud for you. In conclusion, there are many factors that affect your time at work, but you should not be worried or stressed about the uncertain future. I think that's about it. I'd like to thank you all for coming in today. Do you have any questions?

🎧 Case 2

Before we end, let me briefly recap what we have discussed here today. We all have "passion", "energy", "dreams", and "ambition". Our success is dependent on the collective energy and intelligence of all of our team members. Thank you all very much for taking the time to listen to this presentation. Now, if you have any questions, I'd be happy to answer them.

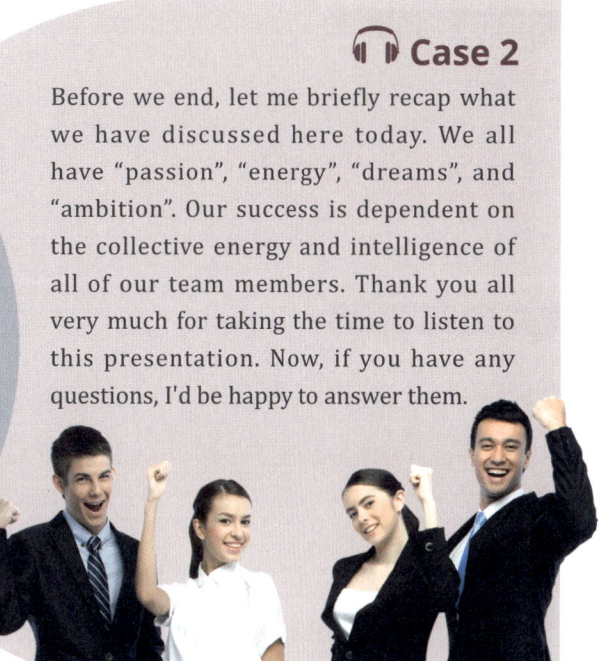

1. Based on the rubric criteria, score the two cases and add up the total score.

Type / Score	Unsatisfactory / 1	Poor / 2	Fair/Average / 3	Good / 4	Excellent / 5
Clear and specific	☐	☐	☐	☐	☐
Connected to main points	☐	☐	☐	☐	☐
Memorable and impressive	☐	☐	☐	☐	☐
Naturally organized	☐	☐	☐	☐	☐

» Case 1 Score :

» Case 2 Score :

2. Which presentation case do you think is better? Support your opinion and discuss it with your partner.

| **Step 3** | **Follow Up**

Use the good case presentation from the previous page. Then write down key points for each of the following categories.

Closing Signal

1

Focused Delivery

2

Call to Action

3

Ending Statement

4

Did You Know?

The final Touch:
Use words & body language to show that you're done

Pause before your final sentence and make it strong and declarative. End with a powerful conclusion such as a call to action or a strong reiteration of your message and its importance to the audience. Even if you end with a rhetorical question, ask it deliberately. Use a strong voice that's loud enough to be heard, make eye contact, stand confidently and smile. When you finish speaking, hold the eye contact and your posture for a few seconds.

Review

1. **Match the correct description with the tips to close your presentation.**

   Movie/Quotation Close •

   Challenge Close •

   Bookend Close •

   Title Close •

   a Engage your audience to apply what you have told them in the speech

   b Refer back to your opening anecdote or quote.

   c Make a reference to a well-known movie.

   d Give your speech a title that expresses your message memorably

2. **Review the examples below. What types of closing techniques were used?**

   1) Let's say your phrase is: "Together, we can win." You repeat that phrase over and over again. Then just before your closing, you say: "I know that all of you are talented, all of you are driven. I know that none of us can do this alone, but together we can win!"

   _____

   2) If you were concluding a speech on the importance of maintaining self-confidence in the face of adversity, you could say, "We have to be like the bird" –the bird that author Victor Hugo once observed – "the bird that pauses in its flight awhile, on boughs too light, – on a branch that is likely to break– feels that branch break, yet sings, knowing she hath wings."

   _____

3. **For additional listening practice, you may listen to good case mp3 or read the script below and complete the sentences.**

   Before we end, **a** _____ here today. We all have "passion", "energy", "dream", and "ambition". Our success is dependent on **b** _____ of all of our team members. Thank you all very much for **c** _____ to this presentation. Now, if you have any questions, I'd be happy to answer them.

Answer Key: ⓐ let me briefly recap what we have discussed ⓑ the collective energy and intelligence ⓒ taking the time to listen

Presentation On Stage

Step 1 — Presentation Practice

You are a campus recruiter looking for young developers for startups on the East Coast. This fall, startups are sponsoring a nationwide tour that kicks off September 30th. Your speech to students is for finding engineers and helping them realize their dreams.

◎ **Who is the audience, and what is the purpose of the speech?**

The speech targets computer science and engineering students at 25 top campuses, including Cornell, Princeton, Penn State, MIT and Harvard. It aims to reach 20,000 students. One of the goals of the tour is to tell the students the story about their options outside of giant corporations such as Goldman, McKinsey, and the Ford Motor Company.

» **In the box below, write down the key points you want to deliver in your conclusion.**

· Key Points to include in your conclusion

✓ Checklist for Effective Conclusions

- ☐ Alert the audience that the speech is ending.
- ☐ Devote no more than 1/6th of the entire presentation to the conclusion.
- ☐ Reiterate the main points.
- ☐ Remind listeners of the speech topic and purpose.
- ☐ Challenge the audience to respond to your ideas or appeals.
- ☐ Make a final statement and make a lasting impression..

Step 2 | Evaluate Yourself & Others

Mark △ for yourself and mark ○ to evaluate others.

Evaluating Presentation Performance

Closing Signals	1	2	3	4	5
· Linking connection of ideas					
· Appropriate structure					
· Complete sense of closure					

Focused Delivery	1	2	3	4	5
· Voice					
· Posture					
· Gestures					
· Eye contact					

Language	1	2	3	4	5
· Audience invited to a call to action					
· Main points properly reminded					
· Proper length					

Overall	1	2	3	4	5
· Main point reiterated					
· Proper examples					
· Appropriate visual aids					
· Well-managed ending statement					

» Your Score: _____   » Others: _____

Let's Recap!

Check to see if you have used any of the phrases from the Phrase Bank.

*Remember! Using these phrases will help you deliver a more effective presentation.

◆ **Signposting the end of your presentation.**
- ☐ At this stage I would like to run through / over the main points…
- ☐ This brings me to the end of my presentation.
- ☐ So, as we have seen today…
- ☐ As a result we suggest that…
- ☐ In the light of what we have seen today I suggest that…
- ☐ In conclusion I would like to say that…
- ☐ I would like to finish by reminding everyone that…

◆ **Linking ideas, and sections/making transitions**
- ☐ In conclusion…
- ☐ To summarize… / To sum up…
- ☐ Let's sum up, shall we?
- ☐ Let's summarize briefly what we've looked at…
- ☐ Finally, let me remind you of some of the issues we've covered…
- ☐ If I can just sum up the main points…
- ☐ Before I stop, let me go over the key issues again.
- ☐ What I've tried to show in this part…
- ☐ To recap what we've seen so far…

The Golden Rules for Unit 8

End Your Presentation on a High Note

6 Ways to Close Your Presentation

1. **Bookend Close**
   Refer back to your opening anecdote or quote and say, "We have arrived, now, where we began." Then reiterate the message you want your audience to remember.

2. **Challenge Close**
   Challenge your audience to apply what you have told them in the speech.

3. **Title Close**
   Give your speech a provocative title that encapsulates your message memorably.

4. **Sing-song Close**
   Ask the audience to repeat a phrase that you used several times in your speech. Let's say your phrase is: "Together, we can win." You repeat that phrase over and over again.

5. **Callback Close**
   Refer back to a story you told where some activity was not fully completed. Then pick up the story and close it around your theme.

6. **Movie / Quotation Close**
   Make a reference to a famous movie / book / quotation to harness the audience's attention, much like turning on a spotlight.

Thinking it Over

1. Which of these tips do you find most useful? Does your partner have the same answer as you?

2. What tips can people use to turn a dull ending into a strong ending?

Opening the Floor

In Unit 9, you will learn how to…
- deal with questions effectively
- keep credibility established during a presentation
- anticipate unexpected questions

Getting Started
Describe the picture within 1 minute using your own words.

Warm-up Questions
1. What advice do you have for handling questions during presentations?

2. What do you do when you don't know the answers to an audience member's question?

Unit 09

Opening the Floor

1. FYI: Background Knowledge

Don't let the Q&A take you down!

Be prepared.
Write down **questions you anticipate** may be asked, especially the **tough or controversial** ones. Run through **a mock session** with some trusted colleagues. They always come up with unexpected questions.

Be confident.
Smile and look your questioners in the eye. The **eye contact** shows that you are focusing carefully on the question and the questioner. The **smile** is an invitation to friendship and connection.

Pause.
If you need a moment before answering a question, take it. Audiences usually appreciate that you **take your time** to consider the questions, and it won't feel like a scripted answer.

Don't fidget.
Scratching your nose, blinking excessive, moving around, and displaying other **nervous tics** signal that you're uncomfortable. Work to **minimize these twitches**.

Answer the Question Straight.
Presenters sometimes don't answer questions that are asked because they weren't listening closely enough or didn't know the answer and decided to talk about something tangential they had expertise on instead. Nothing **erodes the credibility** you've built with the audience more than avoiding the questions.

Confirm you answered the question.
Occasionally ask "Does that answer your question?" or "Is that clear?" It shows your audiences you want to make sure **their needs are being met**.

Practice. Let's recap background knowledge.

1 Make sentences using the chucks from the article above.

a) take one's time: _____

b) look somebody in the eye/eyes: _____

c) erode credibility: _____

2 Match the words with their correct meanings.

- anticipate • • a) move or act in a nervous or restless way
- controversial • • b) a period of time in which something is stopped before it is started again
- pause • • c) likely to produce argumentative controversy
- fidget • • d) to think of something that will or might happen in the future

3 Create a 1-minute speech using the following words.

a) fidget / erode credibility / take one's time (Topic: Bad habits)

_____

Score: ___/10	Used all 3 words (5 pts)	Consistency (3 pts)	Length of the speech (2 pts)

b) controversial / anticipate / pause (Topic: How to resolve disagreements)

_____

Score: ___/10	Used all 3 words (5 pts)	Consistency (3 pts)	Length of the speech (2 pts)

2. Language Focus

Useful Words & Expressions

- Below are expressions and phrases that will help you construct effective presentations.
- Review the expressions and try to use them in the presentation practice section.

✓ If the question is on-topic:
- That's a good question, and we'll come back to it at the end.
- Good question, but I'm not sure. Does anyone in the audience know? I'm not sure off the top of my head, but I bet you can find the answer in/on _____.
- That's a great question, and I'd love to know the answer myself. I'll look into it and get back to you.
- That's a great question, but I'm not sure. My gut says …

✓ If the question is off-topic:
- That's an interesting question, but that's not my area of expertise. Does anyone else happen to know?
- That's a little off-topic for right now, but I bet it will make for an interesting discussion once we wrap up. If anyone has any insight into this person's question, be sure to see him or her afterward.

✓ Dealing with difficult question:
- **Playing for time**
  That's an interesting/difficult point/question/comment/point of view/ I'm glad you raised that point.
- **Avoiding giving answers**
  Perhaps we could deal with this later. Can we talk about this on another occasion? I'm afraid that's not my field. I don't have the figures with me. I'm sure Mr/Ms.... could answer this question. I'll get back to you if time permits.

Listed below are useful expressions for handling questions after a presentation. Try to use them during your presentation practices.

Phrase Bank

Clarifying questions

- I'm afraid I didn't quite catch that.
- If I could rephrase your question…
- Could you repeat your question, please?
- Does this answer your question?

Dealing with difficult questions

- Just a minute please.
- How can I put it?
- I'm glad you asked that question.
- That's a good question/point/remark.
- Can I answer that question later?
- That is a question for an expert.
- Actually, I'd prefer not to discuss that today.
- I'm afraid I don't know the answer to your questions, but I'll try to find out for you.
- Sorry, I don't know that off the top of my head.

1 Match the most appropriate answer to the sample situations below.

An audience member asks a question in the middle of a presentation.	An audience member asks you a nitpicky detailed question.	The presenter thinks an audience member could briefly answer the question.
a	**b**	**c**
1	**2**	**3**
That's an interesting question, but that's not my area of expertise. Does anyone else happen to know?	I'm not sure off the top of my head, but I bet you can find the answer in / on _____.	That's a good question, and we'll come back to it at the end.

3. 3 Steps Building Up

Case Study: How to Handle Questions

| Step 1 | Prep-Stage

Read the case study context and the situation. Answer the comprehension questions and brainstorm presentation ideas.

The Context			Real Situation
The Company	**The Presenter**	**The Audience**	**The Presentation**
Design Co. is the leading wholesale clothing company. After a soft launch of the new denim line this year, the company decided to release the whole collection next year. During the market week, Dean Kemp, the sales director, has invited potential customers to present their next year's Spring collection.	Dean Kemp is the sales director at Design Co. He's waiting for potential customers visiting from the San Francisco Bay Area. The customers are interested in their next year's denim collection, on which he is giving a presentation.	Customers own retail stores all around the nation. They plan to present the new denim line in a dedicated section at the stores. The key pieces that the retailers are interested in are the blue denims for men's in clean and authentic washes.	Dean spent more time on the main part of the presentation than the budgeted time. Customers were ready to ask critical questions as Dean realized he ran over his allotted time. Q&A will either have to become a rushed afterthought, or it won't happen at all.

1. What are the steps that need to be taken in order to prepare a well-planned Q&A session?

✎

✎

✎

✎

2. How would you deal with difficult questions when you are running out of the budgeted time?

✎

✎

✎

✎

Step 2 | Case Comparison

In step 2, read the two Q&A session cases. Then determine which one you think is better.

🎧 Case 1

Presenter: So, I've just summarized what I've covered before the Q&A session. Now it's time to open it up for your questions.

Customer: I know this is not really relevant to the topic this time, but I have a question for you. I am just wondering if you can tell me where I can find small boutique shops around this area. I'd like to check out the latest trends.

Presenter: The problem is that we are running out of time, and I don't have time for irrelevant questions at this point because I'll have to close this presentation in 3 minutes. Does anyone else have any other questions before we wrap up this session?

Case 2 🎧

Presenter: So, I've just summarized what I've covered before the Q&A session. Now it's time to open it up for your questions

Customer: I know this is not really relevant to the topic this time, but I have a question for you. I am just wondering if you can tell me where I can find small boutique shops around this area. I'd like to check out the latest trends.

Presenter: That's a little off-topic for right now, but I bet it will make for an interesting discussion once we wrap up. If anyone has insight into her question, be sure to see her afterward. If you have any other questions that you come across later on, please do not hesitate to drop me a line. My email is…

1. Based on the rubric criteria, score the two cases and add up the total score.

Type	Unsatisfactory	Poor	Fair/Average	Good	Excellent
Score	1	2	3	4	5
Welcome the questions	☐	☐	☐	☐	☐
Clarify the questions	☐	☐	☐	☐	☐
Take time to think before answering	☐	☐	☐	☐	☐
Reply positively	☐	☐	☐	☐	☐

» **Case 1 Total Score** :

» **Case 2 Total Score** :

2. Which presenter does better handling questions? Case 1 presenter? or Case 2 presenter? Write down your reasoning.

3. Work in pairs. Read the two cases. As your partner reads, note what the presenter does well and poorly. Use the checklist.

Step 3 | Follow Up

Use the good Q&A session from the previous page. Write down key points for each of the following categories.

Did You Know?

Don't end with "ANY QUESTIONS?"

If at all possible, avoid taking questions at the very end of your presentation - doing so shifts the energy away from you and can also result in a negative conclusion, especially if you get an off-base or hostile question which you have to reply to defensively. You also have lost the benefit of a strong close if the questions just trail off into silence and you have to say, "...ok, no more questions?"

Review

1. Match the correct description with the tips to close your presentation.

Ground Rules	Parking Lot	Budget Your Time	Prime the Pump
a Give your speakers a firm stopping point before starting a Q&A session.	**b** Establish a parking lot for difficult questions and get back to your audience later.	**c** Set ground rules before you open it up to Q&A.	**d** Engage your audience to ask first few questions.

2. Prepare a Q&A session using the following phrases. Work in pairs.

① Can I answer that question later?
»

② That's a good question/point/remark.
»

③ I'm afraid I don't know the answer to your questions.
»

3. Fill in the blanks to complete the Q&A conversation.

Presenter So, I've just summarized what I've covered before the Q&A session.
_____. (Invite questions)

Customer _____. (Politely bring out the question)
I am just wondering if you can tell me where I can find small boutique shops around this area. I'd like to check out the latest trends.

Presenter _____. (Politely avoid giving answers)
If anyone has insight into her question, be sure to see her afterward. If you have any other questions that you come across later on, please do not hesitate to drop me a line. My email is…….

Presentation
On Stage

Step 1 **Plan a Presentation**

You are a production manager at a wholesale clothing company, and you are visiting a factory to have a production meeting for next year's collection. You will be giving a presentation during the meeting, and at the end, the factory managers will ask questions for more technical details.

◎ **Audience**

You work in the factory production team and will attend the meeting to get the fundamental guidelines for next year's collection. It's now time to begin the Q&A session.

» **Scenario 1.**
Ask a question that is on-topic.
   a) Clarify the question.
   b) Check if the question is satisfied.

» **Scenario 2.**
Ask a question that is off-topic.
   a) Clarify the question.
   b) Play for time.
   c) Avoid giving answers (or say you don't know).

» **Write the questions in the box.**

· Scenario 1

· Scenario 2

✓ **Checklist for Dealing with Questions**

☐ Welcome the question
☐ Take time to think before answering
☐ Clarify the question
☐ Accept criticism positively
☐ Reply positively
☐ Check whether the questioner is satisfied

Step 2 | Evaluate Yourself & Others

Mark △ for yourself and mark ○ to evaluate others.

Evaluating Presentation Performance

Listen	1	2	3	4	5
· Welcome questions					
· Give all of your attention					
· Maintain steady eye contact					

Understand	1	2	3	4	5
· Take time to think before answering					
· Clarify questions					
· Reflect back to confirm understanding					

Communicate & involve	1	2	3	4	5
· Accept criticism positively					
· Keep your tone sincere and nonjudgmental					
· Use appropriate and polite language					

Respond	1	2	3	4	5
· Reply positively					
· Check whether the questioner is satisfied					

» Your Score: _____   » Others: _____

Let's Recap!

Check to see if you have used any of the phrases from the Phrase Bank.

*Remember! Using these phrases will help you deliver a more effective presentation.

◆ **Clarifying questions**
- ☐ I'm afraid I didn't quite catch that.
- ☐ If I could rephrase your question…
- ☐ Could you repeat your question, please?
- ☐ Does this answer your question?

◆ **Dealing with difficult questions**
- ☐ Just a minute please.
- ☐ How can I put it?
- ☐ I'm glad you asked that question.
- ☐ That's a good question/point/remark.
- ☐ Can I answer that question later?
- ☐ That is a question for an expert.
- ☐ Actually, I'd prefer not to discuss that today.
- ☐ I'm afraid I don't know the answer to your questions, but I'll try to find out for you.
- ☐ Sorry, I don't know that off the top of my head.

The Golden Rules for Unit 9

5 Tips to Set the Stage for a Smooth, Yet Captivating Q&A Session

1. **Set Expectations from the Start**
   Before you introduce speakers, let the audience know that there will be time at the end of the session for Q&A.

2. **Ground Rules**
   Before you open the floor to Q&A, it's helpful to set a few ground rules. For example: Wait for the microphone before asking your question. No self-promoting preludes. Introduce yourself and then get straight to the question.

3. **Manage Your Time**
   Give your speakers a firm stopping point, after which you'll open the floor for Q&A.

4. **Prime the Pump**
   Many people wait for that first question to be posed before jumping into the mix. It helps to enlist a few brave souls in advance.

5. **Parking Lot**
   Some folk go off-topic or ask tough questions that might require additional research. Establish a parking lot for these questions and let your audience know that you'll post answers to these questions online at a later time.

(Donna Kastner; Event Planning; http://blog.cvent.com)

Thinking it Over

1. How and when do you tell the audience there will be a Q&A session at the end of the presentation?

2. List three strategies that you can use to maintain control during the Q&A time of a presentation.

Informative Presentations

In Unit 10, you will learn how to…
- give an informative presentation effectively
- guarantee reliable delivery of messages
- build and maintain credibility throughout a presentation

Getting Started

Dean's family cook a big meal together every weekend. They believe it gives their children a healthier life. What are some other ways to keep your body healthy? Present for at least 1 minute.

Warm-up Questions

1. List 3 things that you do to warm up before giving an informative presentation?

2. How do you get audience's attention to start/end an informative presentation?

Unit 10

Informative Presentations

1. FYI: Background Knowledge

Creating an Informative Presentation

An informative presentation is a common request in the business and industry. It's **the verbal and visual equivalent of a written report.** Information sharing is part of any business or organization. Informative presentations serve to **present specific information for specific audiences for specific goals or functions.** Informative presentations are often **analytical** or involve the **rational analysis** of information. Sometimes they simply "report the facts" with no analysis at all, but still need to communicate the information in a clear and concise format.

Tailor your message to the audience

An informative presentation does not have to be a formal event, though it can be. It can be generic and nonspecific to the audience or listener, but the more you know about your audience, the better you can deliver your message. When **you tailor your message** to your audience, you zero in on your target and increase your effectiveness. The emphasis is on **clear and concise communication,** but it may address several key questions:

- ✓ Topic: Product or Service?
- ✓ Who are you?
- ✓ Who is the target market?
- ✓ What is the revenue model?
- ✓ What are the specifications?
- ✓ How was the information gathered?
- ✓ How does the unit work?
- ✓ How does current information compare to previous information?

Practice. Let's recap background knowledge.

1 Fill in the blanks using the bolded words and expressions from the article above.

a) An informational presentation is common request in business and industry. It's the _____ and _____ equivalent of a written report.

b) When you _____ to that audience, you zero in on your target and increase your effectiveness.

c) Informative presentations serve to present specific _____ for specific _____ for specific _____ or functions.

d) Informative presentations are often _____ or involve the _____ of information.

2 Match the words with their correct meanings.

analytical •   • a) giving a lot of information clearly and in a few words
concise •   • b) dividing into elemental parts or basic principles
specific •   • c) based on or in accordance with reason or logic
rational •   • d) clearly defined or identified

3 Create a 1-minute speech using the following words.

a) rational / analytical / tailor one's message (Topic: How to become a good leader)

_____
_____
_____

Score: /10	Used all 3 words (5 pts)	Consistency (3 pts)	Length of the speech (2 pts)

b) concise / specific / equivalent of (Topic: What makes you unique)

_____
_____
_____

Score: /10	Used all 3 words (5 pts)	Consistency (3 pts)	Length of the speech (2 pts)

2. Language Focus

Useful Words & Expressions

- **Below are expressions and phrases that will help you construct effective presentations.**
- **Review the expressions and try to use them in the presentation practice section.**

◆ An informative presentation is a presentation with a main point or purpose that gives information. Informative speeches **describe, define, analyze, tell how to use, and synthesize**:
- I will describe what it's like to be…
- I will define…
- I will analyze the reasons why…
- I will tell how to use…
- I will synthesize the views of…

◆ To maintain credibility, it is also crucial to say why your topic/talk is relevant for your audience:
- Today's topic is of particular interest to those of you / us who…
- My talk is particularly relevant to those of you / us who…
- My topic is / will be very important for you because…
- By the end of this talk, you will be familiar with…

◆ Be sure to provide your audience with detailed purposes – *Don't be vague.*
- The purpose / objective / aim of this presentation is to…
- Our goal is to determine how / the best way to…
- What I want to show you is…
- Today I'd like to give you an overview of…
- Today I'll be showing you / reporting on…
- I'd like to update you on / inform you about…
- During the next few hours, we'll be…

1 Prepare a complete sentence using the following phrases.

a) I will analyze the reasons why

b) By the end of this talk, you will be familiar with

c) During the next few hours, we'll be

Phrase Bank

The list below are useful expressions for giving informative presentations. Try to use them during your presentation practices.

Inviting questions

- I'd be happy to answer any questions…
- If there are any questions, please feel free to ask.
- If there are any suggestions or comments, feel free to speak up.
- Now I'll try to answer any questions you may have.

Thanking the audience

- Many thanks for your attention.
- Thank you all for being such an attentive audience.
- Thank you all for listening.

3. 3 Steps Building Up

Case Study: Social Networking Websites and How They Work

| Step 1 | Prep-Stage

Read the case study context and the situation. Answer the comprehension questions and brainstorm presentation ideas.

The Context			Real Situation
The Company	**The Presenter**	**The Audience**	**The Presentation**
Broadcaster.com is a live webcam social network. It provides its users with a wide range of services, including Broadcaster News created by its own reporters. Broadcaster filters out all the uunnecessary information on big websites like CNN and Facebook. Broadcaster views itself as the next-generation community site that will outdo YouTube or MySpace in quality and popularity.	Christine Quigley is a social media marketing manager at Broadcaster.com, which is a live webcam social network. The purpose of her presentation this time is to deliver information on social networking websites and how they work.	The site's users exchange their opinions in chat groups, create personal profiles, post pictures, and have a sense of belonging. Broadcaster is an entertainment community of about one hundred thousand users, ten percent of whom are logged in. They feel that what they desperately need is good advice about how social networking websites work and how to use them effectively.	Christine is giving an informative presentation to the active site users on how networking websites work. Christine is going to give the audience some crucial tips that they should know to use the social networking sites effectively in a time-efficient way.

1. How do you overcome stage fright? What skills do you need to work on to have a great stage presence?

    🖉

    🖉

    🖉

    🖉

2. Read the context of the presentation. Imagine you are making the presentation.

    a) What content will you include?
    b) How will you structure the content?
    c) Rehearse with your team members and get additional ideas for a better presentation.

    🖉

    🖉

    🖉

    🖉

| Step 2 | Case Comparison

Read the two case presentations and determine which one is more effective.

🎧 Case 1

In a borderless culture, networking is cultural mobility. Social networking guarantees communication, interaction, and social exchange of ideas, beliefs, and opinions without leaving your home. It becomes a remedy from loneliness and boredom. Social networking websites are countless. You may be surprised at the huge number of users. You might already be a user of one of these popular websites. It may be too late for you to try new options, so you might think you are wasting your time.

🎧 Case 2

Social networking has gained popularity with Internet users, and I believe, all of you are Internet users. Surfing the Internet is very time-consuming. We all feel that what we desperately need is good advice about how to use social networking websites in a time-efficient way. Social networking websites offer you an online community to share and explore common interests and activities. They typically provide a variety of ways for you to interact: through chat, messaging, email, video, voice chat, file-sharing, blogging, forums, discussion groups, and applications. Now let's face the facts. Although we have our favorites, it is always good to try new options, like a small social networking website, such as Broadcaster.com.

1. **Read the two cases and fill out the chart. Then determine which case you think is better.**

	Case 1	Case 2
Topic		
Purpose		
Target Audience		
Which case do you think is better?		

| **Step 3** | **Follow Up**

Choose any topic to brainstorm for an informative presentation. Use the brainstorming boxes below.

Topic

Purpose

Target Audience

How to Approach

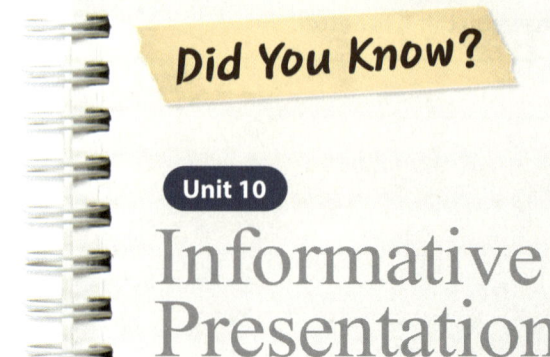

Did You Know?

Unit 10
Informative Presentation

The Final Touch:
Slow Down, You're Talking Too Fast!

When most people are nervous, they will want to talk faster than they usually do. Fight this instinct with all your might. Either that, or prepare 35 minutes worth of content for a 30 minute speech. If you don't speed up when you're nervous, disregard this item.

Review

1. **Match the presentation topics with the correct examples.**

   Definitional Presentation —○   ○— a) How you negotiate and buy a car for a discount price.

   Descriptive Presentation —○   ○— b) A manager wants to inform employees about a new workplace Internet use policy.

   Explanatory Presentation —○   ○— c) The meaning of civil rights has changed significantly over time. What does it mean today compared to the 1960s?

   Demonstrative Presentation —○   ○— d) How to Survive if You Get Stranded in the Wilderness.

2. **Connect the expressions to its category and complete the sentences.**

   · State the main purpose.
   · Maintain credibility: Why is the presentation relevant for the audience?
   · Provide the audience with detailed purposes.

   ⓐ I will describe what it's like to be _____ .

   ⓑ What I want to show you more in depth is _____ .

   ⓒ My talk is particularly relevant to those of us who _____ .

3. **For additional listening practice, you may listen to good case mp3 or read the script below and complete the sentences.**

   Social networking has gained popularity with Internet users, and I believe, you all are internet users (Smile and Pause).

   ⓐ _____ . We all feel that what we desperately need is good advice about how to use social networking websites ⓑ _____ . Social networking websites ⓒ _____ and explore common interests and activities. They typically provide a variety of ways for you to interact: through chat, messaging, email, video, voice chat, file-sharing, blogging, forums, discussion groups, and applications. Now let's face the fact. ⓓ _____ , it is always good to try new options, like a small social networking website, broadcaster.com.

Answer Key: ⓐ Surfing the internet is very time-consuming. ⓑ in a time efficient way. ⓒ offer you an online community to share ⓓ Although we have our favorites.

Presentation On Stage

Step 1 — **Presentation Practice**

You are an emergency room physician and medical school professor. You also serve on the board of directors for a local non-profit cancer organization. You are preparing a speech about "How to Beat Cancer" for World Cancer Day.

◎ **Who is the audience, and what is the purpose of the speech?**

The county invites the local residents to attend the event on World Cancer Day. The presentation is scheduled for 11 a.m. in the college auditorium. Your speech is about raising general public awareness on cancer problems and training audience members on how to prevent and control cancer.

» **Brainstorm: List ways to prevent cancer.**

1.
2.
3.
4.

✓ Checklist for Informative Presentations

- ☐ **Purpose and Topic:** Clear purpose, appropriate and narrowed topic
- ☐ **Audience Analysis:** Adapts to audience characteristics, interests, attitudes, etc.
- ☐ **Credibility:** Believable, trustworthy, competent, committed, etc
- ☐ **Logistics:** Adapts to occasion and place of presentation, including use of equipment
- ☐ **Content:** Includes a variety of interesting and valid supporting material
- ☐ **Organization:** Clear organization and key points, effective introduction and conclusion, clear transitions
- ☐ **Performance:** Appropriate form(s) of delivery, effective vocal and physical delivery, including eye contact
- ☐ **Presentation Aids:** Effective choice, design, and handling of presentation aids
- ☐ **Informative Strategies:** Appropriate and effective strategies, clear delivery of message

Step 2 | Evaluate Yourself & Others

Mark △ for yourself and mark ○ to evaluate others.

Evaluating Presentation Performance

Purpose and Topic	1	2	3	4	5
· Clearly stated					
· Appropriate for audience					

Audience analysis	1	2	3	4	5
· Target Audience					
· Specific information properly prepared					

Credibility	1	2	3	4	5
· Reliable / trustworthy information					
· Confident statements					
· Established audience rapport					

Content	1	2	3	4	5
· Well researched					
· Broad / detailed enough					
· Content relevant					
· Appropriate for the audience					

Organization	1	2	3	4	5
· Carefully planned					
· Coherent					
· Clear					
· Well-timed					

Performance	1	2	3	4	5
· Appropriate gestures					
· Appropriate tone of voice					
· Eye contact					

Overall	1	2	3	4	5
· Message clearly delivered					
· Objective achieved					
· Enjoyable and interesting					
· Effective choice of visual aids					

» Your Score: _____

» Others: _____

Let's Recap!

Check to see if you have used any of the phrases from the Phrase Bank.

* Remember! Using these phrases will help you deliver a more effective presentation.

◆ **Inviting questions**

☐ I'd be happy to answer any questions…

☐ If there are any questions, please feel free to ask.

☐ If there are any suggestions or comments, feel free to speak up.

☐ Now I'll try to answer any questions you may have.

◆ **Thanking the audience**

☐ Many thanks for your attention.

☐ Thank you for being such an attentive audience.

☐ Thank you all for listening.

The Golden Rules for Unit 10

Types of Informative Presentations

Definitional Presentations

The speaker attempts to set forth the meaning of concepts, theories, philosophies, or issues that may be unfamiliar to the audience. Regardless of the listeners' level of knowledge about the subject, it is very important in these types of speeches to show the relevance of the topic to their lives.

Explanatory Presentations

An explanatory presentation is similar to the descriptive speech in that they both share the function of clarifying the topic. Explanatory speeches focus on reports of current and historical events, customs, transformations, inventions, policies, outcomes, and options.

Descriptive Presentations

The purpose of descriptive presentations is to provide a detailed, vivid, word picture of a person, animal, place, or object and determine the characteristics, features, functions, or fine points of the topic. Audiences should carry away in their minds a clear vision of the subject.

Demonstrative Presentations

The most practical of all informative presentations, a demonstration presentation shows listeners how some process is done or how to perform it themselves. The focus is on a chronological explanation of some process, procedure, application or course of action.

Thinking it Over

1. Have you experienced giving an informative speech / presentation? If yes, what types of informative speeches do you find most useful?

2. What types of informative presentations seem easier / harder than other types to prepare?

Persuasive Presentations

In Unit 11, you will learn how to...
- understand the audience's perception of the topic or subject
- shape your information to specifically address the audience's needs
- convince the audience to agree with an idea or opinion

Getting Started

Steven is sitting at his desk throwing his arms up in the air and shouting with glee at his success. What just happened to him? Why is he so excited? Share your opinions and thoughts in your own words.

Warm-up Questions

1. Clarify the differences between an informative speech and a persuasive speech.

2. Why is speaking to persuade especially challenging?

Unit 11

Persuasive Presentations

1. FYI: Background Knowledge

Guide to Persuasive Presentations

Persuasive presentations are not exactly easy. Generally, people are pretty stubborn when it comes to what they believe. Luckily, a few simple tips and tricks can help you give an excellent, sensitive, informed, credible, and inspiring persuasive speech with relative ease.

Get the audience on your side.

People don't like to be talked at; they like to be talked to. **Include the audience in what you're saying**; you can ask questions from the general audience or a specific person. **Make the audience feel involved and important**, and you're more likely to get them on your side.

Stay organized.

If you're all over the place with your speech, people aren't likely to trust you and they certainly aren't likely to be persuaded by your argument. **Keep your thoughts organized** and always return to your main point. This will not only make your position clearer, but your organized delivery will allow **the audience to better understand your position.**

Stay honest and credible.

Don't bite off more than you can chew. **Stay honest and to the point.** Don't hide information or display any other type of bias in your speech. If the audience asks questions or has concerns, **answer honestly.** Display integrity and **have your arguments backed by evidence.**

Consider the other positions on the issue.

Your goal isn't to prove another position wrong; it's to get people to start **considering your point of view.** Don't attack or belittle other opinions. In fact, **establish common ground,** and then explain why you believe your opinion makes more sense.

Practice. Let's recap background knowledge.

1 Fill in the blanks using the above bolded words and expressions.

a) Your goal isn't to prove another position wrong; it's to get people to start _____.

b) Make the audience _____, and you're more likely to get them on your side.

c) Keep _____ and always return to your main point.

d) Display integrity and have _____.

2 Use the chunks from the article to make sentences.

a) take ... into account:

b) get someone on one's side:

b) establish / get / find common ground:

3 Work in groups. Make a list of things you can do to make an audience feel involved during a persuasive presentation.

e.g. Ask questions from the general audience or a specific person.

a)

b)

c)

2. Language Focus

Phrase Bank

Listed below are useful idioms and expressions that you can use in your persuasive presentations.

Above board
- If anything is described as **above board**, it is open, honest, and legal.

Hold all the aces
- A person or company who **holds all the aces** is in a very strong position because they have more advantages than anyone else.

Signed, sealed, and delivered
- When an agreement, contract, or treaty is **signed, sealed, and delivered**, all the legal documents are in order.

Sell ice to Eskimos
- This expression is used to describe a person who has the ability to persuade someone to accept something totally unnecessary or useless.

Leave the door open
- If you **leave the door open**, you behave in such a way that allows the possibility of further action.

Useful Words & Expressions

Common Persuasive Words and Phrases: Strengthen Your Presentations

- Review the expressions and try to use them in the presentation practice section.

ⓐ Agreement
- I agree…
- I am convinced that …

  e.g. I'm convinced that it would be to your advantage to join.

ⓑ Strong Agreement
- I strongly believe you should know that…
- I have no doubt…
- It will be clearly seen…
- I agree wholeheartedly…

  e.g.1 I agree wholeheartedly with him on the new scenario.

  e.g.2 I have no doubt that the new program will bring major success by offering consumers something special.

ⓒ Disagreement
- It would be a disservice…
- I fail to agree…

  e.g. Diplomats failed to agree on details for the peace talks.

ⓓ Strong Disagreement
- I strongly oppose…
- I find it offensive…

  e.g. I strongly oppose the new tax legislation.

ⓔ General Acceptance
- goes without saying…
- stands to reason…
- speaks for itself/themselves…
- It is obvious to say…

  e.g.1 It goes without saying that you are to wear formal clothing to the White House dinner.

  e.g.2 It stands to reason that a child who is constantly criticized will grow up to have no self-confidence.

  e.g.3 Your results speak for themselves. You need to work harder.

Work in Pairs

1. Pick a debatable social issue to discuss with your partner. Use the expressions from above to persuade your partner.

2. Was your partner convincing? Give feedback to each other.

3. 3 Steps Building Up

Case Study: Confident Delivery: Emotional Appeal

| Step 1 | Prep-Stage

Read the case study context and the situation. Answer the comprehension questions and brainstorm presentation ideas.

The Context			Real Situation
The Company	**The Presenter**	**The Audience**	**The Presentation**
L'Oréal is a leading total beauty care company based in Paris, France. Their main goal is providing affordable luxury for people who demand excellence in beauty. Their slogan, 'Because I'm Worth It', has been what the brand stands for since 1973, and today the company focuses on more women recognizing and responding to this positive phrase and powerful sentiment.	Patricia Li is the marketing product manager at L'Oréal Canada. She is delivering her persuasive presentation before they unveil their new makeup line this coming Friday.	Anybody who can help spread the word about the product is invited to the product launch event: Relevant groups include journalists, industry analysts and potential customers. Also invitees should be credible people with some product/industry authority that can rate and give reviews that will generate interest.	The purpose of the launch is to spread the word about the new product by gaining media coverage and building consumer credibility at the same time. Patricia is pretty confident it's pretty convincing since L'Oréal has already spread the word through social media networks such as Facebook, LinkedIn and Twitter in very effective ways to reach their target audience. Live tweeting has proven to be an effective method of emotional appealing between interested groups.

1. **What is the hardest thing about trying to persuade people to come to your side? What do you do when you meet a stubborn person who is not willing to give in?**

   ✎

   ✎

   ✎

   ✎

2. **Imagine that you are Patricia about to give presentation about the new makeup product. What different effective persuasive approaches would you use on the following audiences?**

   a. A boss
   b. A peer
   c. A challenging person
   d. An open-minded person

Step 2 | Case Comparison

Read the two case presentations and determine which one is more effective.

🎧 Case 1

It seems obvious that all beauty brands use concepts that somehow relate to either inner or outer beauty. Of course, that's the reason why we purchase and consume beauty products in the first place, right? So, I'd simply like to tell you to use our products for soft skin. The new line focuses on bright and shiny with highlighted dark color contrasts. It indicates freshness, cleanness, and youth.

🎧 Case 2

Shake up your look! because you're worth it! L'Oréal Canada offers a complete head-to-toe range of cosmetics. We have the know-how and product performance to give you what you need. You'll feel worth it with sophisticated nail polish colors, a flawless foundation base, and eye looks perfect for any occasion. Whether you need your everyday cover-up or you're getting ready for a night out, explore our range to discover your perfect match.

1. **Based on the rubric criteria, score the two cases and add up the total score.**

Type	Unsatisfactory	Poor	Fair/Average	Good	Excellent
Score	1	2	3	4	5
Makes audience feel involved	☐	☐	☐	☐	☐
Appeals emotionally	☐	☐	☐	☐	☐
Stays organized	☐	☐	☐	☐	☐
Sound honest and credible	☐	☐	☐	☐	☐

» **Case 1 Total Score** : 　　　　　　» **Case 2 Total Score** :

2. **Which case do you think is better? Support your opinion and discuss it with your partner.**

/ Unit 11. Persuasive Presentations /

| **Step 3** | **Follow Up**

Brainstorm for a persuasive presentation. With your class, or on your own, choose any topic to persuade your audience. Brainstorm your ideas in the boxes below.

Topic

1

Pupose

2

Target Audience

3

How to Approach

4

Did You Know?

Unit 11 Persuasive Presentation

The Final Touch:
Emotion is an essential element of persuasion.

Too often people shy away from emotion in presentations, thinking that it's not appropriate. Nothing could be further from the truth. Human beings make important decisions emotionally and only afterward justify their behavior with rational arguments. First, understand the mood or emotional climate of the situation. Then, bring appropriate emotional language into your talk.

Review

1. **Create a 1 minute speech using the following expression.**

   ⓐ Sell ice to Eskimos (Topic: Try to market a product that nobody wants)

   _____
   _____

Score: ___/10	Used the given expression (5 pts)	Persuasive (3 pts)	Length of the speech (2 pts)

   ⓑ Hold all the aces (Topic: How to advance in your career)

   _____
   _____

Score: ___/10	Used the given word (5 pts)	Persuasive (3 pts)	Length of the speech (2 pts)

2. **Identify which type of persuasive presentation claim is used in the following sentences.**

   Value Claims   **Policy Claims**   **Factual Claims**   **Definitional Claims**

   a) _____ : An advertisement is not a work of art because when it becomes one, it loses its purpose of selling.

   b) _____ : The United States should become independent from the use of foreign oil.

   c) _____ : It's unfair for pregnant women to have special parking spaces at malls, shopping centers, and stores.

   d) _____ : The tallest man in the world, Robert Wadlow, was eight feet and eleven inches tall.

3. **For additional listening practice, you may listen to good case mp3 or read the script below and complete the sentences.**

   L'Oréal Canada offers a complete ⓐ _____. We have the know-how and product performance to ⓑ _____. You'll feel worth it with sophisticated nail polish colors, ⓒ _____, and perfect looking eyes for any occasion. Whether you need your everyday cover-up or ⓓ _____ explore our range to discover your perfect match. Now, does your skin feel more comfortable, attractive, self-confident, and BEAUTIFUL?

   Answer Key : ⓐ head-to-toe range of cosmetics ⓑ give you what you need ⓒ a flawless foundation base ⓓ you're getting ready for a night out

Presentation On Stage

Step 1 **Plan a presentation**

You are a team leader who believes that smoking contributes to absenteeism and lost productivity. You're planning to propose a smoke-free workplace starting next year. It will be tough to get employees to support this plan because 75% of employees smoke.

◎ **Who is the audience, and what is the purpose of the presentation?**

The majority of employees will attend the presentation. The purpose of this presentation is to persuade your audience members that breaking the habit of smoking is the right way to go, because smoking is harmful to the smoker's own self, as well as to others.

» **Write your key persuasive points the box below.**

· Key Persuasive Points
1.

2.

3.

✓ Persuasive Presentations Checklist

☐ **Purpose and Topic:** Clear purpose, reasonable goals, appropriate and narrowed topic

☐ **Audience Analysis:** Adapts to audience characteristics, interests, attitudes; adapts to different types of listeners

☐ **Credibility:** Believable, trustworthy, competent, committed, charismatic

☐ **Logistics:** Adapts to occasion and place of presentation, including use of equipment

☐ **Content:** Includes valid arguments supported by strong evidence and reasoning

☐ **Organization:** Clear and strategic organization, effective introduction and conclusion, clear connectives

☐ **Performance:** Appropriate form(s) of delivery, effective vocal and physical delivery, including eye contact

☐ **Presentation Aids:** Effective choice, design, and handling of presentation aids

☐ **Informative Strategies:** Appropriate and effective strategies, clear delivery of message

Step 2 | Evaluate Yourself & Others

Mark △ for yourself and mark ○ to evaluate others.

Evaluating Presentation Performance

Purpose and Topic	1	2	3	4	5
· Clearly stated					
· Appropriate for audience					

Audience analysis	1	2	3	4	5
· Target Audience					
· Specific information properly prepared					

Credibility	1	2	3	4	5
· Reliable / trustworthy information					
· Confident statements					
· Established audience rapport					

Content	1	2	3	4	5
· Well researched					
· Broad / detailed enough					
· Content relevant					
· Appropriate for the audience					

Organization	1	2	3	4	5
· Carefully planned					
· Coherent					
· Clear					
· Well-timed					

Performance	1	2	3	4	5
· Appropriate gestures					
· Appropriate tone of voice					
· Eye contact					

Overall	1	2	3	4	5
· Message clearly delivered					
· Objective achieved					
· Enjoyable and interesting					
· Effective choice of visual aids					

» **Your Score:**

» **Others:**

Let's Recap!

Check to see if you have used any of the phrases from the Phrase Bank.

* Remember! Using these phrases will help you deliver a more effective presentation.

◆ **Above board**
☐ If anything is described as above board, it is open, honest, and legal.

◆ **Hold all the aces**
☐ A person or company who holds all the aces is in a very strong position because they have more advantages than anyone else.

◆ **Signed, sealed, and delivered**
☐ When an agreement, contract, or treaty is signed, sealed, and delivered, all the legal documents are in order.

◆ **Sell ice to Eskimos**
☐ This expression is used to describe a person who has the ability to persuade someone to accept something totally unnecessary or useless.

◆ **Leave the door open**
☐ If you leave the door open, you behave in such a way that allows the possibility of further action.

The Golden Rules for Unit 11

Types of Persuasive Presentations

① Value Claims

The speaker advocates a judgment claim about something.
(e.g., it's good or bad, it's right or wrong).

- Dating people on the Internet is an immoral form of dating.
- SUVs are gas-guzzling monstrosities.

② Policy Claims

Policy claims will always have a clear and direct opinion for what should occur and what needs to change. Policy claim is probably the most common form of persuasive speaking because we live in a society surrounded by problems and people who have ideas about how to fix these problems.

- The tobacco industry should be required to pay 100 percent of the medical bills for individuals dying of smoking-related cancers.
- The United States needs to invest more in preventing poverty at home and less in feeding the starving around the world.

③ Factual Claims

Factual claims set out to argue the truth or falsity of an assertion. All factual claims are well-documented by evidence and can be easily supported with a little research.

- Barack Obama is the first African American President it the United States.
- Facebook wasn't profitable until 2009.

④ Definitional Claims

Definitional claims are claims over the denotation or classification of what something is. Most definitional claims fall into a basic argument formula:

X is (or is not) a **Y** because it has (or does not have) feature(s) **A**, **B**, and / or **C**.

- The lottery is really a tax on the poor.
- Nicotine is not a dangerous drug.

Thinking it Over

1. What other methods can be used to grab the attention of the audience other than just using words?

2. Have you ever talked about a topic which you're an expert on with someone who isn't? /Suggestion:

Refine & Rehearse

In Unit 12, you will learn how to…
- make your rehearsal more productive
- use rehearse time more efficiently
- rehearse to master stage presence

Getting Started

Keith has videotaped his presentation rehearsal. What is he doing during the rehearsal at the auditorium? Share your opinions and thoughts in your own words.

Warm-up Questions

1. How much time do you spend rehearsing your presentation?

2. What do you work on the most when you rehearse presentations?

Unit 12

Refine & Rehearse

1. FYI: Background Information

How to Make Your Rehearsal More Productive

Do you end up rehearsing in front of your audience? Rehearsal is **an important final step** in the process of mastering your material and developing a sense of timing. Most people know they should prepare and rehearse presentations, but end up doing a quick mental run-through and feel that is enough. Attention to delivery is usually postponed until the last minute.

- **Rehearse mentally.** Review your speech from start to finish in your head several times. See yourself being successful. Most athletes spend as much time preparing themselves mentally as they do physically.

- **Memorize** the opening and closing lines of your speech.

- Select an organizational pattern that will keep you and the audience on track. **Make an outline** of your main and supporting points.

- **Rehearse on site** so that you have home-court advantage. Sit in the back of the room. Become aware of your surroundings and how you will appear to the audience.

- Conduct a **dress rehearsal.** If your presentation requires more **formal attire** such as a suit and tie for man, or heels for woman, rehearse wearing these clothes.

- Plan on **finishing your graphics a few** days early. Know the **exact sequence** and how you will present each slide.

- Rehearse from beginning to end. **Time yourself** so that you **finish 2 minutes early.**

- **Videotape yourself.** Get feedback.

Practice. Let's recap background knowledge

1 Fill in the blanks using the above words and expressions in bold.

a) _____ so that you have home-court advantage. Sit in the back of the room.

b) If your presentation requires _____ such as a suit and tie for man, or heels for woman, rehearse wearing these clothes.

c) _____. Review your speech from start to finish in your head several times.

d) Rehearse from beginning to end. _____ so that you finish 2 minutes early.

2 Use the chunks from the article to make sentences.

a) keep … on track:

b) quick run-through:

c) home-court / field advantage:

3 Work in groups. Make suggestions on how to rehearse a presentation.

e.g. Practice in front of trusted friends, family, or colleagues.

a)

b)

c)

2. Language Focus

Phrase Bank

Listed below is a review of expressions from unit 1-12. Remind yourself again and try to use them in your presentation practices.

Introduction
- I'd like to start by introducing myself. My name is…
- I'm here today to present…
- My presentation will take about 30 minutes.
- I'll ask you to save your questions until the end.

The Main Part
- There are three things we have to consider: one, two, and three. (or A, B, and C.)
- On the plus side, we can add…
- Let's consider this more in detail.
- Now we'll move on to…

Describing Visuals
- As you can see here…
- The chart / slide / table / graph on the following slide shows…
- To illustrate this, let's have a closer look at…
- This graph clearly shows…
- From this, we can understand how / why…
- I'd like us to focus our attention on…

Conclusion
- At this stage I would like to run through/over the main points…
- Let's summarize what we've looked at…
- Finally, let me remind you of some of the issues we've covered…
- If I can just sum up the main points…
- Before I stop, let me go over the key issues again.
- To recap what we've seen so far…

Q&A Time
- I'm glad you asked that question.
- If I could rephrase your question…
- Could you repeat your question, please?
- Does this answer your question?

Useful Words & Expressions: Idioms in Presentations

Idioms are expressions that have a meaning different from the dictionary definitions. Because English contains many idioms, non-native English speakers have difficulties making logical sense of idioms and idiomatic expressions. The more you are exposed to English, however, the more idioms you will come to understand. Until then, memorizing the more common idioms may be of some help.

Idiom	Definition	Sentence
a blessing in disguise	a good thing you do not recognize at first	Losing my job was a blessing in disguise.
a piece of cake	easy to do	Our team is strong, but it won't be a piece of cake to make it to the finals.
better late than never	it is better to do something late than not at all	A: I'm sorry I'm late for the meeting. B: Better late than never, right?
get over it	recover from something (like a perceived insult)	Get up, get over it, and move on!
not a chance	it will definitely not happen	A: Will classroom volunteers solve America's reading problems? B: Not a chance.
on pins and needles	very nervous about something that is happening	I've been on pins and needles all day, waiting for you to call with the news.
the sky is the limit	the possibilities are endless	You can do anything you set your mind to, Billy. The sky's the limit.

Work in Pairs

1 Test your partner to see if he or she memorized all the idioms.

2 Choose 3 idioms from above and create sentences using the idioms.

3. 3 Steps Building Up

Case Study: Boost Overall Presentation Quality

| Step 1 | Prep-Stage

Read the case study context and the situation. Answer the comprehension questions and brainstorm presentation ideas.

The Context			Real Situation
The Company	**The Presenter**	**The Audience**	**The Presentation**
NVS is a multinational pharmaceutical company based in Switzerland. The company came up with new insomnia products and just got FDA approvals. The head of NVS recently decided to limit advertising and plan a low-budget promotional event.	David Epstein is the head of NVS Pharmaceuticals. He is giving a promotional presentation during the event. NVS has been under pressure to keep coming up with promising products due to expiring patents. NVS hopes this turns out to be a strong opportunity to market the new products.	The company invites new investors to the promotional event. Some are experienced investors and others are just getting into the field. The audience members get to familiarize themselves with the company.	The purpose of the presentation is to give new investors opportunities to learn about the company's growth strategy, meet the management team, and find information on key products commercially available and in the development pipeline.

1. Try to develop your own model outline for the presentation.

   ✎

   ✎

   ✎

   ✎

2. Discuss in pairs. How would you engage the audience (new investor)? What message would you give them?

   ✎

   ✎

   ✎

   ✎

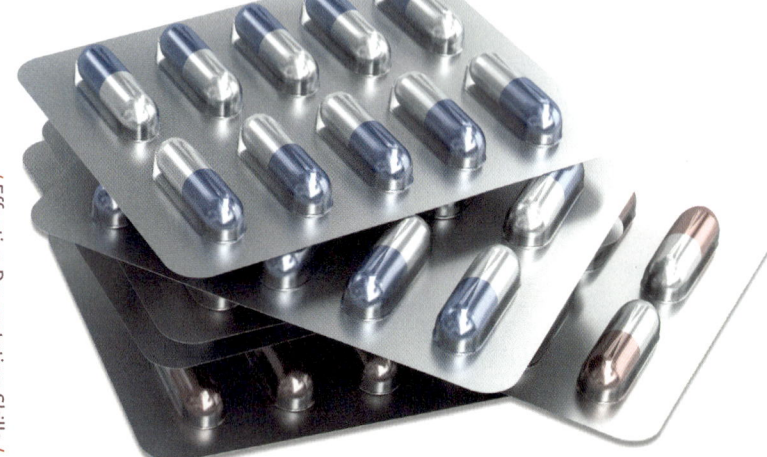

| Step 2 | Case Comparison

Read the two case presentations and determine which one is more effective.

Case 1
The opening of the presentation

Start with a slide with the statistic you want to use and say to the audience "Hands up all of you who got a great night's sleep last night?" After some audience members raise their hands, you then introduce your statistic "My name is David, and I'm here today to talk about some promising products. Let's get back to '1 in 3.' It is estimated that 1 in 3 people in the world will suffer from insomnia, and we have been researching ways of reducing this number, which is great news for those of you who didn't put your hands up!"

Case 2
The closing of the presentation

Finally, let me remind you of some of the issues we've covered today. We recognize that the next two years will be challenging in the pharmaceutical industry, and we are proactively making these changes to further focus our product lines on the best opportunities and align our market position on our growth brands. These are difficult but necessary decisions that will free up resources to invest in the future of our business, which we view as well-suited to bring new valuable therapies to patients and payers. Now let me turn the time over to a Q&A session.

1. Based on the rubric criteria, score the two cases and add up the total score.

Type / Score	Unsatisfactory / 1	Poor / 2	Fair/Average / 3	Good / 4	Excellent / 5
Stated topic and title	☐	☐	☐	☐	☐
Organized clearly	☐	☐	☐	☐	☐
Sounds competent and trustworthy	☐	☐	☐	☐	☐
Introduced/concluded effectively	☐	☐	☐	☐	☐
Appropriate for the audience	☐	☐	☐	☐	☐
Provided summary of the main points	☐	☐	☐	☐	☐

» **Opening Presentation** Total Score :

» **Closing Presentation** Total Score :

2. What did the presentations do well, and didn't do well. Support your opinion and discuss it with your partner.

| **Step 3** | **Follow Up**

Work in Pairs Read the topic and write a 3-minute short presentation. Use the brainstorming box below.

» **Topic:** How to help the team cope with stress

Did You Know?

The Final Touch: Rehearse & Shine!

Rehearse your presentation out loud in real time, and enjoy an 80% advantage over other presenters, because they're not rehearsed.

To take your presentations to champion level, here is a shortcut: At a minimum, rehearse once in real time. Here's another shortcut: Rehearse each section of your presentations for five minutes. Rehearse the opening of your presentation and see how far you get in five minutes. Those first five minutes will also reveal your comfort level with your material. By rehearsing in short increments, you will be able to do the quickly determine the length your presentation.

Review

1. **Create a 5-minute speech on the given topic. Try telling a personal story to help the audience grasp the concept easily.**

   a How to overcome cultural barriers at work

   ....

   ....

Score: /10	Organized well (5 pts)	Used a personal story (3 pts)	Length of the speech (2 pts)

   b How to meet deadlines easily

   ....

   ....

Score: /10	Organized well (5 pts)	Used a personal story (3 pts)	Length of the speech (2 pts)

2. **Fill in the blanks reviewing the presentation tips.**

   a Take time to _____. It will give the audience _____ with you and digest.

   b Wait for the attendee to _____ before you start to answer.

   c Remember, you are _____, no matter how technical the information is.

   d Each slide should be displayed for at least _____, and no longer than _____.

3. **For additional listening practice, you may listen to good case mp3 or read the script below and complete the sentences.**

   Finally, let me remind you of some of ⓐ _____ today. We recognize that the next two years will be challenging in the pharmaceutical industry, and we are proactively ⓑ _____ to further focus our product lines on the best opportunities and align our market position on our growth brands. These are difficult but necessary decisions that will ⓒ _____ in the future of our business, which we view as well-suited to bring new valuable therapies to patients and payers. Now ⓓ _____ a Q&A session.

   Answer Key : ⓐ the issues we've covered ⓑ making these changes ⓒ free up resources to invest ⓓ let me turn the time over to

Presentation On Stage

Step 1

Plan a Presentation

You are a labor union leader at an IT company, and always try to understand what the employees really need. This is generally achieved through employee surveys, but can also be done using focus groups or meetings with various employee groups. Recently company employees are becoming increasingly vocal in protecting their rights and requesting flexible working hours.

◎ Who is the audience, and what is the purpose of the presentation?

A majority of audience members are the employees who are willing to meet with union leaders and address their concerns in the workplace. You will be speaking at the conference on the effectiveness of flexible working hours and how such an arrangement would meet their needs.

» **Brainstorm ideas:**
Write down key points you want to include in each section.

· Introduction

· Body

· Conclusion

✓ Overall Presentations Performance Checklist

☐ Objectives   ☐ Content   ☐ Organization   ☐ Visual Aids

☐ Delivery   ☐ Language   ☐ Overall

/ Effective Presentation Skills /
128

Step 2 | Evaluate Yourself & Others

Mark △ for yourself and mark ○ to evaluate others.

Evaluating Presentation Performance

Objectives	1	2	3	4	5
· Clearly stated					
· Appropriate for audience / subject					

Content	1	2	3	4	5
· Well researched					
· Broad / detailed enough					
· Content relevant					
· Appropriate for the audience					

Organization	1	2	3	4	5
· Carefully planned					
· Coherent					
· Clear					
· Well-timed					

Visual Aids	1	2	3	4	5
· Appropriate for subject and audience					
· Legible and structured					
· Introduced and explained well					
· Supported overall message					

Delivery	1	2	3	4	5
· Rate of speech and quality					
· Established audience rapport					
· Eye contact					
· Appeared confident and positive					
· Used body to emphasize meaning					
· Clearly audible					

Language	1	2	3	4	5
· Clear					
· Accurate					
· Appropriate					
· Well-pronounced					
· Used signaling phrases					

Overall	1	2	3	4	5
· Clear message					
· Achieved objective					
· Interesting					
· Enjoyable					
· Informative					
· Motivating					

» Your Score: » Others:

Let's Recap!

Check to see if you have used any of the phrases from the Phrase Bank.

*Remember! Using these phrases will help you deliver a more effective presentation.

◆ **Introduction**
- ☐ I'd like to start by introducing myself. My name is…
- ☐ I'm here today to present…
- ☐ My presentation will take about 30 minutes.
- ☐ I'll ask you to save your questions until the end.

◆ **The Main Part**
- ☐ There are three things we have to consider: one, two, and three. (or A, B, and C.)
- ☐ On the plus side, we can add…
- ☐ Let's consider this more in detail.
- ☐ Now we'll move on to…

◆ **Describing Visuals**
- ☐ As you can see here…
- ☐ The chart / slide / table / graph on the following slide shows…
- ☐ To illustrate this, let's have a closer look at…
- ☐ This graph clearly shows…
- ☐ From this, we can understand how / why…
- ☐ I'd like us to focus our attention on…

◆ **Conclusion**
- ☐ At this stage I would like to run through / over the main points…
- ☐ Let's summarize what we've looked at…
- ☐ Finally, let me remind you of some of the issues we've covered…
- ☐ If I can just sum up the main points…
- ☐ Before I stop, let me go over the key issues again.
- ☐ To recap what we've seen so far…

◆ **Q&A Time**
- ☐ I'm glad you asked that question.
- ☐ If I could rephrase your question…
- ☐ Could you repeat your question, please?
- ☐ Does this answer your question?

The Golden Rules for Unit 12

What to Focus on When Rehearsing a Presentation

Timing and Content
- Each slide should be displayed for at least ten seconds, and no longer than two minutes.
- Each concept should have three to four statements to support it.
- Practice your presentation, and remember that practice usually runs 20% faster than your actual presentation.

During Your Presentation
- Fold back the upper corner of your notes so pages can be turned easily.
- Prepare your script with cues for yourself (smile, pause here, eye contact, etc.).
- Speak in a friendly, relaxed manner.
- Remember, you are telling a story. Try using personal examples, no matter how technical the information is.
- State your objectives at the beginning of your presentation.
- Track your time to avoid running over time.
- Have a prepared and memorable summary.
- Give credit to others who contributed.
- Take time to pause. It will give the audience time to catch up with you and digest.

Question & Answer
- Repeat each question so that the entire audience hears it.
- Take a moment to reflect on the questions.
- Wait for the attendee to finish his or her entire question before you start to answer.
- Use the last question to summarize.

Thinking it Over

1. What methods do you use to stay relaxed during a presentation?
2. How does telling personal stories help audiences and presenters?

Effective Presentation Skills
Answer Key

Answer Key

Unit 1 Paving the Way for Presentation

Practice. Let's recap background knowledge

1 Chunk Study (model answers)
  ⓐ Inspiring presentations have shaped the world because they brought on meaningful changes.
  ⓑ Some presenters employ this power to persuasively act on them.
  ⓒ A good presentation can be demonstrated by the manner in which it is delivered.

2 Match the words
  · Credibility – ⓒ
  · Persuasively – ⓐ
  · Distinguished – ⓓ
  · Essential – ⓑ

3 Fill in the blanks
  ⓐ responsible, unethical
  ⓑ essential, persuasively
  ⓒ to deliver, inspiring

Review

1 Match the presentation types
  ⓐ talk
  ⓑ workshop
  ⓒ demonstration
  ⓓ product launch

2 Place right expressions according to its category
  · Welcoming the audience – ⓐ, ⓒ
  · Introducing your subject – ⓑ, ⓕ
  · To get the audience's attention – ⓓ, ⓔ

Unit 2 Understanding Your Audience

Practice. Let's recap background knowledge

1 Fill in the blanks
  ⓐ get straight to the point
  ⓑ critical thinking about logistics
  ⓒ jargon
  ⓓ interrogatives
  ⓔ has several practical advantages

2 Match the words
  · Who – ⓓ
  · Where – ⓐ
  · When – ⓒ
  · How – ⓑ

3 True or false
  ⓐ F   ⓑ T   ⓒ T

Useful Words & Expressions

1 Fill in the blanks
  ⓐ notably
  ⓑ keep in mind
  ⓒ in detail
  ⓓ what do you think

Review

1 Audiences & Logistics: Unscramble the words
  ⓐ Understanding and adapting to your audience has several practical advantages.
  ⓑ A thorough understanding of your audience can help you focus your presentation and decide how to narrow your topic.
  ⓒ Adapting to the place where you will be speaking requires critical thinking about logistics.

2 Connect the expression
  · Big Room Presentation Skills – ⓑ, ⓒ
  · Structured Group Dynamic Skills – ⓓ, ⓗ
  · Interactive Training Skills – ⓕ, ⓖ
  · Small Group Facilitation Skills – ⓐ, ⓔ

3 Put them in order
  ⓐ 1   ⓑ 3   ⓒ 2

Unit 3 Let's Get Started

Practice. Let's recap background knowledge

1 Fill in the blanks
  ⓐ primary effect
  ⓑ at its peak
  ⓒ audience, focus their attention
  ⓓ simultaneously, feel for the audience, last-minute adjustments

2 Short answers (model answers)
  ⓐ Introduction gives the audience time to adjust, settle in, block out distractions, and focus their attention on to you and your message while allowing the presenter to feel for audience, calm down and make any last-minute adjustments.
  ⓑ It means that beginning of the presentation is the point at which audiences' attention to new stimulus is at its peak. Therefore introduction is important as this period is where the audience is highly focused.

3 True or false
ⓐ T　　ⓑ F　　ⓒ T　　ⓓ T

Useful Words & Expressions
1 Choose either more formal (M) or less formal (L)
ⓐ M　　ⓑ L　　ⓒ L　　ⓓ M

Review
1 Effective Introductions: Unscramble the words
ⓐ The main purpose of the introduction is to introduce your topic to the audience.
ⓑ You can create a positive lasting impression and pave the way for a presentation that achieves your purpose.
ⓒ A good introduction establishes a relationship among three elements: you, your message and your audience.

2 Connect the expression
- Essential element – ⓐ, ⓓ
- Unnecessary element – ⓑ, ⓒ

3 Fill in the blanks
ⓐ ladies and gentlemen
ⓑ welcome you today
ⓒ let me start by introducing myself
ⓓ topic of today's presentation

Unit 4 Linking the Parts

Practice. Let's recap background knowledge
1 Effective Organization: Unscramble the words
ⓐ The point of deductive approach is to gather ideas and pass them onto the audience.
ⓑ Inductive approach is good to use when you want to get the audience to participate.
ⓒ In a combination approach, you suggest instances, events or issues and ask your audience to help you determine the principle.

2 Choose type of organization approach.
ⓐ C　　ⓑ I　　ⓒ D

3 True or false
ⓐ T　　ⓑ T　　ⓒ F

Useful Words & Expressions
1 Fill in the blanks using linkers.
ⓐ However　　ⓑ In particular　　ⓒ Similarly

Review
1 Organization Basics: Fill in the blanks
ⓐ pass it onto, little room for
ⓑ audience to participate, consensus
ⓒ reach a conclusion, based on the group

2 Connect the different phrases
ⓐ 3　　ⓑ 5　　ⓒ 1　　ⓓ 2　　ⓔ 4

3 Organization Tools: Short answers (model answers)
ⓐ Deductive, inductive and combination
ⓑ Gives you a clear and logical framework on which you hang your ideas and supporting material.

Unit 5 A Picture is Worth A 1000 Words

Practice. Let's recap background knowledge
1 Fill in the blanks
ⓐ intensifying persuasiveness.
ⓑ suitably selected
ⓒ visual communication

2 True or false
ⓐ T　　ⓑ F　　ⓒ T

Useful Words & Expressions
1 Fill in the blanks
- Speed of change – ⓑ
- Degree of change – ⓒ
- Describing change – ⓐ

Review
1 connect
ⓐ rose
ⓑ flattened
ⓒ considerably
ⓓ slightly

2 Mark the correct names
ⓐ Line graph
ⓑ Flowchart
ⓒ Bar graph
ⓓ Pie chart

3 Why Visuals? Unscramble the words
ⓐ Pictures are far more superior in the communication capabilities.
ⓑ We can digest information better through pictures.
ⓒ Suitably selected images will greatly increase the effectiveness of the delivery.

Answer Key

Unit 6 Powerful Delivery

Practice. Let's recap background knowledge

1 Chunk Study (model answers)
ⓐ Sometimes genetic advantages make sports unfair.
ⓑ Impromptu storytelling teaches us how to be creative and interesting.
ⓒ If you have a commanding presence, you'll be able to capture the audiences' attention.

2 Match the words
· persistent – ⓒ
· animate – ⓐ
· enlarge – ⓓ
· externalize – ⓑ

Review

1 Match factors of presentation
· Correct – ⓒ
· Simple – ⓐ
· Emotional – ⓓ
· Visual – ⓑ

2 Connect the correct examples of the gestures
· ① – ⓓ
· ② – ⓒ
· ③ – ⓑ
· ④ – ⓐ

Unit 7 Adding a Special Touch

Practice. Let's recap background knowledge

1 Chunk Study (model answers)
ⓐ You have to work long hours and that can put off a lot of people.
ⓑ He was clattering away at his keyboard.
ⓒ I am sure I can make good use of the gift you gave me.

2 Match the words
· phenomenon – ⓓ
· epidemic – ⓑ
· distracted – ⓐ
· spot – ⓒ

Useful Words & Expressions

1 Rewrite sentences using colorful language.
(model answers)
ⓐ Using cellular phones causes no harm inside the hospital.
ⓑ This tends to make log browsing a tedious and ineffective process.
ⓒ My boss trudged towards the door after the conversation.

Review

1 Tools for Engaging Your Audience: Match
· Statistics – ⓓ
· Activities – ⓑ
· Metaphors – ⓒ
· Repetitions – ⓐ

2 Good Case: Complete the sentences
ⓐ hold it in your hands
ⓑ boots in 12 seconds
ⓒ absolutely charismatic
ⓓ Get a close-up look at

3 Phrase Bank: Complete the sentences.
(model answers)
ⓐ As I have already said earlier, don't do what doesn't feel right.
ⓑ Have you ever experienced stage fright? If so, how did you overcome the feeling?
ⓒ Sorry, what I meant was it wasn't so easy for me, either.

Unit 8 Finishing Strongly

Practice. Let's recap background knowledge

1 Chunk Study (model answers)
ⓐ The call to action said Click Here to enter a survey to qualify to win a prize.
ⓑ The bright colors on the poster are there to grab your attention.
ⓒ He straightened the shirt and tucked it into his trousers.

2 Match the words
· critical – ⓐ
· ramble – ⓒ
· obscure – ⓓ
· memorable – ⓑ

Review

1 Match the correct description
- Movie Close / Quotation – ⓒ
- Challenge Close – ⓐ
- Bookend Close – ⓑ
- Title Close – ⓓ

2 Find the types of closing techniques
① Sing Song Close
② Movie / Quotation Close

Unit 9 Opening the Floor

Practice. Let's recap background knowledge

1 Chunk Study (model answers)
ⓐ Bill is very careful and takes his time so he won't make any mistakes.
ⓑ Look me in the eyes and tell me the truth.
ⓒ The CFO warned that low rates would erode the bank's credibility.

2 Match the words
- anticipate – ⓓ
- controversial – ⓒ
- pause – ⓑ
- fidget – ⓐ

Useful Words & Expressions

1 Match the most appropriate answer
ⓐ An audience member asks a question during the meat of your presentation. – ③
ⓑ An audience member asks you a nitpicky detail question – ②
ⓒ The presenter thinks an audience member could briefly answer the question. – ①

Review

1 Match the correct description
- Ground Rules – ⓒ
- Parking Lot – ⓑ
- Budget Your Time – ⓐ
- Prime the Pump – ⓓ

3 Complete the Q&A session
① Now it's time to open it up for your questions.
② I know this is not really relevant to the topic this time, but I have a question for you.
③ That's a little off-topic for right now, but I bet it will make for a interesting discussion once we wrap up.

Unit 10 Informative Presentations

Practice. Let's recap background knowledge

1 Fill in the blanks
ⓐ verbal / visual
ⓑ tailor your message
ⓒ information / audiences / goals
ⓓ analytical / rational analysis

2 Match the words
- analytical – ⓑ
- concise – ⓐ
- specific – ⓓ
- rational – ⓒ

Useful Words & Expressions

1 Match the most appropriate answer
ⓐ I will analyze the reasons why Google Plus Marketing has become a significant player in the social media marketing.
ⓑ By the end of this talk, you will be familiar with the new ERP system.
ⓒ During the next few hours, we'll be discussing the goals for the next project.

Review

1 Match the correct example:
- Definitional Presentation – ⓒ
- Descriptive Presentation – ⓐ
- Explanatory Presentation – ⓑ
- Demonstrative Presentation – ⓓ

2 Connect and complete the expressions
- State the main purpose
  – ⓐ .. conducting a meeting without preparation.
- Maintain credibility
  – ⓒ .. have just graduated
- Provide audience detailed purposes
  – ⓑ .. how to create an employee-friendly work environment.

Answer Key

Unit 11 Persuasive Presentations

Practice. Let's recap background knowledge.

1 Fill in the blanks using the bolded words and expressions.
ⓐ considering your point of view
ⓑ feel involved and important
ⓒ your thoughts organized
ⓓ your arguments backed by evidence

2 Use the chunks from the article to make up sentences.
ⓐ We will take your long years of service into account when we make our final decision
ⓑ The CFO tried to get the higher-ups on his side.
ⓒ The leaders failed to find common ground on the defensive side of this possible bargain.

Review

1 There is no activity needing those answers.

2 Identify which type of persuasive presentation claim is used in the following sentences.
ⓐ Definition Claim
ⓑ Policy Claim
ⓒ Value Claim
ⓓ Factual Claim

3 For additional listening practice, you may listen to good case mp3 or read the script below and compete the sentences.
ⓐ head-to-toe range of cosmetics
ⓑ give you what you need
ⓒ flawless foundation base
ⓓ you're getting ready for a night-out

Unit 12 Refine & Rehearse

Practice. Let's recap background knowledge

1 Fill in the blanks
ⓐ Rehearse on site
ⓑ more formal attire
ⓒ Rehearse mentally
ⓓ Time yourself

2 Use the Chunks from the article
ⓐ Please keep this discussion on track. Time is limited.
ⓑ Could you give me a quick run-through of what the referendum question is all about?
ⓒ Most students are familiar with the concept of home-court advantage in college basketball.

Review

2 Fill in the blanks:
ⓐ pause, time to catch up
ⓑ finish his/her entire question
ⓒ telling a story
ⓓ ten seconds, two minutes